Anonymous

Fish, Flesh and Fowl

A Cook Book

Anonymous

Fish, Flesh and Fowl
A Cook Book

ISBN/EAN: 9783744790017

Printed in Europe, USA, Canada, Australia, Japan

Cover: Foto ©Lupo / pixelio.de

More available books at **www.hansebooks.com**

FISH, FLESH AND FOWL

A COOK BOOK

— OF —

*Valuable Recipes, all of which have been thoroughly
and successfully tested*

COMPILED BY

LADIES OF STATE STREET PARISH

PORTLAND
TRANSCRIPT PRINTING HOUSE, 44 EXCHANGE STREET
1894

"The Lord sends meat; the Devil cooks,"
   Of old a proverb was,
What slander on the gentle sex!
   What charge without a cause!

The Woman Question is, no doubt,
   "Where doth my mission lie?
Shall all our aspirations tend
   To pudding, cake and pie?"

Could man be made to comprehend
   The aggravation sore,
Of frosting, roasting, broiling—all
   The varied kitchen lore—

'Twould all come right then, bye and bye,
   Disproved all slanders rife;
We'd get with jubilation,
   Our *Desserts* in this life.

BREAD.

"The Staff of Life."

Bannock. One pint Indian meal scalded with one quart milk, six or eight eggs, a little sugar and salt. Stir in eggs when cool, and bake in hot oven.

Batter. Two eggs, the whites beaten separately, a small cup of flour, the same of milk; mix yolks of eggs, flour and milk into a smooth batter; stir in a teaspoon of butter melted, and a little salt, and one teaspoon of baking powder; the last thing put in the whites of the eggs beaten to a froth; beat gently after the whites are in. Bake well in a buttered tin in a very hot oven.

Blueberry Cake. 1. One quart flour, half a cup butter, one and a half cups white sugar, one cup sweet milk, two teaspoons cream tartar, one teaspoon soda, two eggs, blueberries.

2. One cup milk, three cups flour, one egg, salt, two tablespoons sugar, one of butter, two teaspoons cream tartar, one of soda, one cup blueberries.

Breakfast Cake. Sift together two cups flour, two tablespoons Indian meal, two tablespoons sugar and four even teaspoons baking powder; add one cup sweet milk and two well beaten eggs, a pinch of salt. Bake in large or small tins.

Breakfast Puffs. One pint milk, two eggs, a little salt, teaspoon soda, two of cream tartar, butter size of a walnut, melted; put all into the milk, then stir thoroughly in a pint and a half of flour. Bake in cups.

Brown Bread. 1, Togus. Three cups sweet milk, one cup sour milk, three cups Indian meal, one cup flour, one cup molasses, one teaspoon salt, one of soda dissolved in a little warm water.

2. **Steamed.** Three cups Indian meal, two cups rye meal, one cup flour, four tablespoons molasses, two tablespoons yeast, one teaspoon salt. Stir it up at night with warm water. In the morning add scant teaspoon saleratus. Steam all the forenoon.

3. One heaping coffee cup rye meal and the same of Indian meal; mix together one-half teaspoon salt, molasses enough to make a very stiff dough, into this beat an egg; two scant coffee cups sour milk, two teaspoons soda. If sweet milk is handier use three teaspoons baking powder. Steam three hours and bake one hour.

4. Three cups bread crumbs, rolled fine, three cups corn meal, three cups sour milk, three-fourths cup molasses, four teaspoons soda. Boil molasses and add soda; steam all day as usual.

Buckwheat Cakes. Two cups buckwheat, one of white flour, one-half cup yeast. In the morning add two teaspoons sugar, and one teaspoon soda.

Buns. 1. Three cups milk, one cup yeast, two cups sugar, flour enough to make a stiff batter; rise over night, then add cup butter, cup sugar, nutmeg, teaspoon soda, more flour to make as stiff as bread; after a second rising cut and rise before baking. Currants if you choose.

2. Two quarts dough, one cup sugar, one pint milk (lukewarm), one cup yeast, one cup currants, put all to rise in the afternoon, add flour enough to thicken before bed time. In the morning put in pans to rise before baking.

3. **Cinnamon.** Boil one pint milk and cool till lukewarm, one cup sugar, one cup yeast, tablespoon butter, one tablespoon lard, flour enough to make a stiff dough so that none need to be added in the morning. Let rise over night; when light roll out about an inch thick and spread well with butter; sprinkle over brown sugar and cinnamon; then roll it up and cut off about an inch thick; let rise in pans till very light, and bake in good oven; when done rub over with butter.

California Biscuit. One-half cup sugar, two cups milk, two eggs, piece of butter size of an egg, one quart flour, one teaspoon soda, two teaspoons cream tartar.

Cheese Sandwiches. One hard-boiled egg, one-fourth pound common cheese grated, one-half teaspoon salt, one-half teaspoon pepper, one-half teaspoon mustard, one-half teaspoon sugar, one tablespoon melted butter, one tablespoon vinegar; take the yolk of the egg, put it in a small bowl and crumble it down, put into it the butter, and mix it smooth with a spoon, then add the salt, pepper, sugar, mustard and the cheese, mixing each well; then put in the tablespoon of vinegar which will make it the proper thickness; spread between thin bread and butter or crackers.

Corn Cake. 1. One pint sour milk, one pint Indian meal, one pint flour, two tablespoons sugar, salt, one egg, a small piece of butter, one teaspoon soda.

2. One cup meal, one cup flour, one cup sugar,

butter size of an egg, one cup milk, one-half teaspoon soda dissolved in milk, two teaspoons cream tartar sifted in with flour.

3. One cup Indian meal, one cup flour, one-half teaspoon soda, one teaspoon cream tartar sifted in with meal, teaspoon salt, one egg, without beating, one cup milk, all beaten very thoroughly together for fifteen minutes and bake in round pans twenty minutes.

Corn Bread or Johnny-Cake. One pint of buttermilk or sour milk, one pint corn meal, one egg, one teaspoon soda, one teaspoon salt, two teaspoons sugar or molasses; dissolve the soda in a little warm water and add it the last thing. Bake half an hour in a quick oven.

Bangor Corn Cake. One tablespoon butter, two tablespoons sugar, one egg, one cup flour, one-half cup corn meal, two-thirds cup milk, one teaspoon cream tartar, one-half teaspoon soda.

White Corn Cake. One cup cold boiled rice beaten, then add three eggs; scald one quart milk, stir with the milk one and a third cups of white corn meal, a little salt, then beat all together, have a good one-half cup of butter in the dish you bake in. Bake in hot oven.

Egg Pop-Overs. Three cups flour, three cups milk, three eggs. Beat eggs twenty minutes, add milk and flour. Bake in a quick oven.

Flannel Cakes. To two ounces of butter add a pint of hot milk to melt the butter, a pint of cold milk, five eggs, flour enough to make a stiff batter, teaspoon salt, two tablespoons yeast; set it to rise in a warm place about three hours; butter the griddle and pour on the batter in small cakes.

BREAD.

French Toast. Beat two or three eggs and stir into a pint of milk with a pinch of salt; take thin slices of stale bread and dip into it; as you take out the slices set them on the edge a minute to drain off some of the milk, then brown on both sides on a buttered griddle; lay them in a hot covered dish, and eat with syrup or butter and sugar.

Fried Biscuits. Take spoonfuls of raised dough and fry in hot lard like doughnuts; eat while hot with maple syrup.

Graham Bread. Take equal quantities graham meal and flour, add shortening and yeast, mix stiff as flour bread and treat in the same way.

Graham Rolls. 1. Two cups of wheat meal, one and a half cups flour, salt, three-fourths cup sugar, two and one-half cups sour milk, one teaspoon soda.

2. Two cups graham flour, one cup sweet milk, one cup sour milk, one-half cup molasses, one-half teaspoon salt, one teaspoon saleratus, one egg. Bake in a quick oven in gem pan.

Huckleberry Biscuit. A piece of raised dough the size of an ordinary bowl, two-thirds a cup sugar, one large tablespoon each butter and cream, one-half teaspoon soda; flour to stiffen like biscuit; put in last a pint of berries stirred in carefully so as not to break them; take out with a spoon, roll them in flour and let them rise in a pan before baking in a moderate oven.

Indian Breakfast Cake. Two cups Indian meal, one-third cup flour, two and a half cups sour milk, one egg, and soda to sweeten the milk.

Indian Cake. Two cups meal, one cup flour, one cup cream, one cup milk, two-thirds cup sugar, three eggs, one teaspoon soda, one of salt.

Indian Drop Cake. Three cups meal, one cup flour, one pint sour milk, two eggs, two large spoons butter, one cup sugar, soda enough to sweeten the milk.

Muffins. One cup sweet milk and an iron spoonful extra, three cups flour, one egg, two teaspoons cream tartar, one of soda, butter size of small egg, tablespoon sugar; beat egg, sugar, butter and cream tartar together; stir in part of milk while putting in the flour, dissolve soda in remainder of the milk and stir in after it is well mixed.

2. One egg, pint of flour, one and a half pints milk, teaspoon butter rubbed into the flour, teaspoon cream tartar, half teaspoon soda.

3. **English.** Two quarts flour, one-third of a yeast cake, one teaspoon salt, cold water to moisten; make the dough as stiff as for bread and rise over night; roll out until one-half inch thick; cut with large biscuit cutter; put them on a griddle on the back of the stove till they rise; then move forward to cook, turning over when done one side; remove from the fire when done; cover and allow to stand long enough to be made tender by the steam; split open, butter and serve; or when cold, split, toast and butter.

4. **Graham.** One cup flour, two cups wheat meal, two tablespoons sugar, teaspoon salt, half cup yeast, well mixed. Add half teaspoon soda dissolved in a little milk; not too stiff, almost thin as a batter.

5. **Graham.** One egg, half cup sugar, butter size of an egg, one and a half cups sour milk, one cup wheat flour, one and a half cups graham flour, half a teaspoon soda; bake in hot roll pans.

6. **Indian Meal.** One cup meal scalded in one pint milk, butter size of an egg, tablespoon sugar, salt, one egg, half cup yeast and flour enough for rather a stiff batter; bake in a quick oven.

BREAD.

7. Raised. One pint sweet milk, half cup yeast, two tablespoons sugar, flour enough to make batter a little thicker than for fritters; rise over night; add in the morning two eggs, and bake in a quick oven.

8. Raised. One quart flour, half a teacup yeast, two well beaten eggs, one and a half pints warm milk, half a gill melted butter; let rise, and when light bake in rings well buttered.

9. Rye. One pint sour milk, one pint rye meal, half cup molasses, one egg, one teaspoon saleratus, cup flour. Bake one-half hour.

10. White. One cup milk, one and a half cups flour, one heaping teaspoon baking powder, whites of two eggs, one-fourth cup butter, a little salt; bake in a quick oven.

Pancakes. One egg, one cup milk, one pint flour, half teaspoon soda, teaspoon cream tartar, salt; drop from teaspoon in hot lard; eat with syrup for breakfast.

2. One egg, a little nutmeg, two-thirds cup sugar, one cup milk, teaspoon soda, two cream tartar, three cups flour; drop in hot fat.

Parker House Rolls. Three-quarters cup yeast, three-quarters cup butter, three pints flour, one tablespoon sugar, one teaspoon salt; scald the milk and cool it, rise all day, cut out at night, and rise until morning; bake in a quick oven; fold over the edges, and put a bit of butter between the folds. As biscuit, just as nice with less butter.

Potato Biscuit. At 9 A. M., (if wanted for tea) dissolve one-half yeast cake in one cup warm water, add one cup mashed potato and one cup flour and a little salt; let it rise till noon, then add one-half cup lard, one-third cup sugar, two eggs and flour enough to knead, but do not knead it; let it rise again till 4 o'clock; then knead and form into biscuit and let rise; brush the tops with milk; bake ten or fifteen minutes.

Potato Cakes. Half a dozen common sized potatoes, boiled and mashed smooth, a spoonful flour, two eggs, salt and pepper; stir until quite soft; fry like fritters.

Potato Rolls. Boil one pint of sliced and peeled potatoes, pour off the water, mash fine, add one pint and a half of water, then strain; one-half cup sugar, tablespoon lard, teacup yeast; rise over night; this makes one loaf and a pan of rolls.

Quaker Biscuit. Scald one cupful Quaker rolled oats with one pint boiling water, and let it stand one hour; add one-half tablespoon shortening, a scant half cup molasses, one-half tablespoon salt, one-half yeast cake, dissolved in one-third cup lukewarm water, one quart flour; let rise, shape, rise again and bake in hot oven twenty minutes.

Rice Crumpets. Two cups warm milk, one cup cold boiled rice, one tablespoon white sugar, two tablespoons melted butter, half a cup liquid yeast, flour to make a thick batter, salt to taste; beat the mixture well and let it rise till very light; just before putting into gem pans add a bit of soda dissolved in hot water; serve hot; bake about twenty minutes.

Rusks. Make a sponge of two cups milk, one cup yeast, salt, flour enough for stiff batter; set it to rise at noon; in the evening mix in a cup of butter, two cups sugar, two eggs well beaten; let it stand all night to rise; in the morning mould into cakes, put them into pans so as not to touch; let them rise again, then bake; a little cinnamon may be added if desired.

BREAD. 11

Raised Rye Bread. Pour one cup boiling water on one cup flour; when free from lumps add one heaping cup rye flour, or sifted rye meal, three-fourths cup molasses, a little salt, and scant half yeast cake; mix with three cups lukewarm water, adding flour to form a stiff batter; do this at night. In the morning take out with a spoon enough to fill gem pan, (one dozen); let them rise about ten or fifteen minutes in the pan before baking; to the rest of the dough add a little more flour and a bit of butter and make into loaves; let it rise a little before baking; bake slowly.

Raised Rye Biscuit. Three cups white flour, one cup rye flour, one-half cup sugar, one teaspoon salt, and a pinch of soda all sifted together; rub into this one teaspoon shortening, dissolve one-half yeast cake, and mix altogether with lukewarm milk and water to the consistency of raised dough; let it rise over night; in the morning form into biscuit and let rise again.

Rye Rolls. Two cups rye meal, one cup flour, half teaspoon salt, a scant cup molasses, two full cups butter-milk or sour milk, a heaping teaspoon soda; beat in an egg the last thing; bake in a quick oven in gem pans.

Squash Biscuit. One cup sifted squash, one-half cup sugar, one cup milk, one-half cup yeast, one-half teaspoon saleratus, butter size of a large egg; flour to roll out.

Squash Fritters. One pint sifted squash, one quart milk, three eggs, one teaspoon soda, salt, enough flour to make little stiffer batter than for common fritters.

Squash Gems. One-half cup stewed and sifted squash, one-fourth cup sugar, one cup milk, one egg, two cups flour, one heaping teaspoon baking powder.

Squash Griddle Cakes. One cup sifted squash, one cup sweet milk, one egg, flour enough to make them the right consistency.

Steamed Whole Wheat Loaf. One-half cup molasses, two cups sour milk, one egg, two even teaspoons soda, one even teaspoon salt, three cups (a little scant) of whole wheat flour; steam three or four hours. It may be made with sifted graham meal; it resembles brown bread, but is more easily digested.

Tea Rolls. Boil one cup milk, let it get cold, take one quart flour and rub in one-half tablespoon lard, make a hole in the middle of the flour and pour in the milk, and one-quarter cup yeast, and the same amount of sugar; let this stand over night, in the morning knead it again and form into rolls or biscuits, let it rise until tea time and bake in a moderately heated oven.

Waffles. 1. One quart flour, little salt, large teaspoon butter, two eggs, half cup yeast; let it rise all day.

2. Three pints milk, half cup boiled rice, while hot put in a piece butter size of an egg, half cup yeast, salt, flour to make a stiff batter; beat the egg very light and add the last thing; raise over night or during the day.

3. **German.** Half pound butter stirred to a cream, yolks of five eggs, mixed with half pound of flour, half pint of milk stirred in gradually and lastly the whites of the eggs beaten to a stiff froth and beaten into the butter.

Wheat Gems. Stir slowly into cold water unbolted wheat flour enough to make it the consistency of hasty pudding, a little salt, and bake as muffins in a very quick oven.

Yeast. 1. Splendid. Boil eight large potatoes, mash fine, add one pint boiling water, one cup sugar, nearly half cup salt, stir until dissolved; add one pint cold water, strain through a sieve, add half cup yeast and set to rise ten or twelve hours before bottling. A pinch of hops can be boiled and strained over it with the boiling water.

2. Grate four large sized raw potatoes; have ready one pint boiling water in which a small pinch of hops has been boiled, strain it over the potato; set it on the fire to cook five minutes, then add one-half cup sugar, one-quarter cup salt, one pint cold water, one-half cup yeast, let it rise and cork tight; this yeast will keep good three months.

3. Four raw potatoes, grated; mix with them three spoonfuls flour, a good pinch of hops, with water enough to cover, boil ten minutes; then strain the water onto the potatoes and flour; add one and a half quarts boiling water; when lukewarm add cup yeast, one-half cup sugar, one-fourth cup salt and set away to rise.

SOUPS.

"Now good digestion wait on appetite."
—[SHAKESPEARE.

Stock. Take lean beef and cold water, in proportion of one pound of beef to one quart water; place it in a soup kettle over a good fire; when it boils add cup of cold water and remove the scum; then place the kettle over a moderate fire and let it simmer slowly four or five hours; this stock may be used for all soups in which meat broth is desired.

Black Bean. One pint black beans, soaked over night; in the morning pour off the water, add a gallon of water, with any bones, either of beef or mutton, (very little meat needed), and boil several hours; season with salt and pepper; take off all the fat, strain the soup and let it boil again before serving; cut a lemon in thin slices and put into the tureen and pour the soup upon it; some add cloves and yolks of hard boiled eggs.

Beef. Take sufficient soup stock; boil one onion, one carrot, one quart potatoes, and vegetables to suit taste, in a little water, and strain into the soup stock; add pepper, salt, etc., to suit.

Bouillon. Put a shank of beef (six or seven pounds) into a large pot and cover with cold water; leave on front of stove until it boils, then move it to the back of stove and let it simmer an hour and a half; cut up two carrots, two onions, and half a lemon; salt to taste, and boil until the meat falls from the bones; then strain through a sieve and set in the cold; next day remove every particle of grease that has risen to the top; heat the bouillon and pour into cups, first having a slice of lemon in each cup; season to taste.

Celery. Five heads of celery, one pint good soup stock, three of water, one-half pint cream or rich milk; cut the celery into inch lengths, put on with the water and cook until tender; take out the celery and rub through a sieve; add to the soup stock and cook slowly one-half hour; heat the cream and stir into it one tablespoon flour rubbed into one tablespoon butter, cook five minutes; pour into the celery, heat very hot but not boil, and serve.

Corn. One quart milk, one pint green corn (cut from the cob), two eggs, butter, pepper and salt to suit the taste. Cook half an hour.

Lobster. Three crackers pounded fine, mixed with the tomally, piece butter size of an egg; boil one quart milk, and pour on the paste, stirring all the time until smooth; chop the lobster fine, put into the mixture, and boil, not too long, as it will make it tough. Pepper and salt.

Mock Oyster. Six ripe tomatoes skinned and boiled in a pint of water, and a teaspoon saleratus, then add a quart of sweet milk, and four crackers pounded. Season with pepper and salt.

Noodle. Two eggs, thicken with enough flour to roll out very thin, let dry two hours, roll and cut very thin; boil twenty minutes in chicken already prepared for soup. Season with onions.

Pea. One pint split peas, three quarts water, half pound salt pork, boil three or four hours, adding more water as it boils away.

Potato. Take six good sized potatoes, boil soft, four onions boiled soft; mash both together till smooth; take three pints new milk, piece butter size of an egg, add potatoes and onions; bring to a boiling point, but do not let it boil. Season with salt and pepper.

Tomato. 1. One teaspoon butter, two teaspoons flour, one pint beef stock, one-fourth of a small onion, put butter in frying pan, cut onion in small pieces and brown; add one can tomatoes and cook one hour; pass through sieve, return to fire and add the stock and flour; season with salt, pepper and Worcestershire sauce. Serve hot.

2. One pint cooked tomatoes, one pint water, when boiled add half teaspoon soda; when done foaming, add one quart hot milk; season well with butter, pepper and salt.

3. One pint boiling water, take one can tomatoes, let it come to a boil, then add two tablespoons flour mixed with the juice from the kettle with the tomato; season with sugar (or not), salt, pepper, butter to taste; boil all together twenty minutes, then strain through a fine sieve. Perfectly delicious.

FISH.

*"With hooks and nets you catch us,
 You never regard our pains;
Yet we reward you with dainty food,
 To strengthen your body and brains."*

Baked Cod. Pour boiling water over the fish, and keep hot an hour; then take it off the bone and put in a dish with a quart of milk, half an onion, one-quarter pound butter, very little thickening of flour, little salt, and cover with bread crumbs. Bake an hour and a half.

Baked Fish. Take a fish weighing from four to six pounds, wash clean, season with salt; make a dressing with five crackers rolled fine, one tablespoon butter, one teaspoon salt, little pepper, one-half teaspoon chopped parsley, water enough to make moist, stuff the fish with this preparation, fasten with skewer, cut slits in fish, put in strips of salt pork, dredge with flour. Bake one hour, basting often. Serve with tomato sauce.

Baked Lobster. Two or three lobsters chopped fine, season with pepper, salt and a tablespoon melted butter, one pint milk thickened with a tablespoon of flour, one teaspoon of mustard. Mix all together and bake with cracker crumbs on top.

Baked Shad Roe. Wash and cook three shad roes in boiling water, salted, with one tablespoon vinegar for ten minutes. Place on a buttered plate, cover with tomato sauce and bake thirty minutes, basting twice.

Tomato Sauce. Two tablespoons butter, one tablespoon flour, one teaspoon salt, one teaspoon pepper, one cup stock, one cup strained tomatoes, a few drops onion juice. Very nice.

Devilled Crabs. Make one cup cream sauce with one tablespoon melted butter, one heaping teaspoon flour, one cup hot cream; season with salt, pepper, a little cayenne and half salt spoon mustard, tablespoon parsley; add the yolks of two hard-boiled eggs, rubbed to a paste; with this add one-half can of crabs; fill the shells, cover with buttered crumbs, brown in oven.

Escaloped Lobster. Cut the meat of a three pound lobster into small pieces; melt two tablespoons butter in a sauce pan, add two tablespoons flour, one-half teaspoon salt, one-half teaspoon pepper, few grains of cayenne; when bubbling pour on slowly one pint hot milk or one cup milk, and one cup hot white stock; add the lobster and fill buttered ramequins with the mixture; cover with buttered bread crumbs, bake until brown.

Fillets of Halibut. Wipe and cut into strips one and one-half pounds halibut, sprinkle with lemon juice, salt and pepper, and lay a thin slice of onion on each strip; cover and let stand one-half hour, then remove the onion, dip the strips in melted butter, skewer into shape; place on a plate, dredge with flour, and bake two minutes in a hot oven. Serve with white sauce made with three tablespoons of butter, and three of flour.

Fish Balls. One pint bowlful of raw fish, two heaping bowlfuls of pared potatoes, two eggs, butter the size of an egg, a little pepper; pick the fish very fine, and measure it lightly in the bowl; put potatoes into the boiler and the fish on top of them, cover with boiling water and boil half hour; drain off all the water, mash fish and potatoes together until fine and light; then add the butter, pepper and egg well beaten; drop from a spoon into boiling fat and cook until brown.

Fish Croquettes. One pint of any kind of cold boiled fish, flake very fine, removing all bone and skin; season well with salt, pepper and chopped onion; boil one cup milk, add one tablespoon butter, thicken with one tablespoon flour; mix with the fish and set aside to cool; when cool shape and rub in fine crumbs of bread or cracker, dip into beaten egg, then roll again in crumbs taking care that every part is covered; fry in boiling fat and serve on a hot platter.

Lobster Croquettes. One pint of lobster meat cut fine; season with one salt spoon salt, one of mustard, little cayenne; moisten with one cup thick cream sauce, cool and shape, roll in crumbs, egg and crumbs again, and fry in smoking hot fat. Drain on paper.

Oyster and Clam Fritters. One and a half pints milk, one and a quarter pounds flour, four eggs, whites and yolks beaten separately, whites stirred in last lightly; clams must be chopped small; oysters used whole.

Oysters. 1. Broiled. Roll each oyster in pounded cracker, lay them on an oyster gridiron and broil each side; make a gravy by pouring boiling water on butter and adding salt to taste. Serve hot.

2. Roast. Put a quart of oysters in a basin with their own liquor, and let boil three minutes; season with a little salt, pepper and butter. Serve on buttered toast.

3. Scalloped. Four crackers, two tablespoons butter, teaspoon pepper, one quart oysters; put a layer of oysters with pepper and salt, then a layer of cracker crumbs with butter, until the dish is full. Bake twenty minutes.

Potted Shad. A white stone jar, and one on which vinegar will have no effect is the first requisite; cut the shad in pieces to fit in the jar, with a little salt, pepper and whole cloves between each layer, then pour vinegar over the whole and cover tightly; cook slowly all day in oven; serve when cold. If the vinegar is too strong dilute it.

Salmon Croquettes. One pound can salmon, one cup powdered cracker, one cup cream; salt and pepper, and least touch of nutmeg; roll in cracker crumbs and beaten egg, and again in cracker crumbs and fry.

MEATS.

"God sendeth and giveth both mouth and the meat."

How to Choose Meats. It is always important to know how to choose meat in buying. Ox beef should be of fine grain or fibre, the flesh or lean of a bright red color and firm, the fat white, and distributed throughout the lean; it should not be yellow or semi-fluid. If the meat is entirely lean, it will be tough and its nutritive power is low. Veal is dry if fresh. It should be close-grained. If the meat is moist and flabby it is stale. Mutton should be of a clear, deep pink tint; firm, and with a liberal supply of fat. Fine wether mutton may be recognized by the presence of a small mass of fat on the upper part of the leg. It is more nutricious than ordinary mutton, the darker its tint the finer its flavor. Pork should be of a pale deep pink tint, and the fat very firm. If it is soft or the fat is yellow the meat is bad. If it is semi-fluid the animal has probably been fed on flesh.

Potted Beef. Take a large beef shank and put it into cold water to cover it, boil until perfectly tender, remove bone and cartilage, chop the meat fine and replace it in the kettle with the liquor which should be one quart, let it simmer gently and season with salt, pepper and mace to suit the taste. Press and cut in slices for lunch or tea.

Croquettes. To use up small, nice pieces of meat, chop them fine, and mix bread crumbs, a little broth or gravy, an egg, pepper and salt. Make into cakes and roll in flour, and fry in hot drippings.

Meat Pie. Cut up some good, tender, raw beef or mutton, season with pepper, salt, and if liked one finely chopped onion; boil half dozen good sized potatoes, when done, mash smooth and wet with milk enough to make a dough to make the crust, salt to taste; roll out full half an inch thick, and line a buttered dish large enough to hold the meat; lay in the meat, add a teacup of water or a little less, then roll out a thick crust of the potato, covering the top of the pie at least an inch thick, and bake about an hour and a half.

Meat and Potato Pie. Butter a baking dish; put in layer of cold mashed potatoes, or sliced ones, but if these are used, small pieces of butter must be added; on the potato put a layer of meat cut in small pieces, little salt, pepper and a few rings of onions; then more potato, and in this way fill the dish having the top potato. Before the last layer of potato, pour in any gravy you may have; bake until the potato is a nice brown.

Devilled Ham. One pint boiled ham chopped fine with a good proportion of fat, one teaspoon dry mustard, one tablespoon flour, one-half cup boiling water. Press in a mould and cut in slices.

Roast Lamb and Mint Sauce. Stuff a hind quarter of lamb with fine bread crumbs, pepper, salt and butter; rub the outside with salt, pepper, butter and flour; then roast two hours. Mint sauce:—Chop the mint fine; pour on a little hot water; let it stand on the stove a short time, then add a little vinegar and sugar to taste.

Sausages. Six pounds lean and two pounds fat pork, four tablespoons salt, six of sage, four of pepper, two of cloves.

To Chop Suet. Sprinkle flour over it while chopping, which will prevent the pieces from adhering.

Veal Loaf. 1. Three pounds raw veal, one-quarter pound salt pork (less will do if a little butter is used), chop fine, mix with two eggs, one cup cracker crumbs, three teaspoons salt, two of pepper, one tablespoon sage; press hard into a pudding dish and bake two hours. To be sliced when cold.

2. Three and a half pounds of raw veal, three slices salt pork chopped fine, six crackers pounded fine, two eggs beaten, tablespoon salt, teaspoon pepper, two pinches allspice, one of cloves, knead all together into a loaf, egg it over, put bits of butter on the top and scatter pounded cracker. Bake two hours basting with water.

Minced Veal. Three and one-half pounds of veal chopped fine, four eggs well beaten, four crackers pounded fine, one tablespoon salt, the same of pepper, one-half tablespoon nutmeg, three tablespoons cream or milk, butter the size of an egg. Mix all together in a loaf and bake two hours.

Veal Cutlets. Cut veal into pieces for serving; season with salt and pepper; dredge with flour (or egg and crumbs); brown in salt pork fat; put into stew pan; make brown gravy; season highly with vegetables cut fine or Worcestershire sauce. Pour over meat and simmer till tender (one and one-half hours).

Timbales. Mince and season meat with salt and pepper; add one egg and about one-half as much bread crumbs as meat; make moist enough with gravy and put in thoroughly buttered cups and bake in pan of water or not.

Camelons. Made same as Timbales, but baked in a roll one-half hour and served with tomato sauce around it.

FOWL.

> "And as an ev'ning dragon came,
> Assailant on the perched roosts
> And nests in order rang'd
> Of tame villatic fowl."
> —[Milton.

Chicken Pie. Cut into pieces the chickens, boil in enough water to cover until tender, adding when half done one tablespoon salt; take out chicken, keep warm, and thicken the liquid with one tablespoon each flour and butter rubbed together; add salt and pepper to taste; boil five minutes; take one quart flour, two teaspoons Cleveland's baking powder, little salt and one small cup butter; mix as biscuit. Take half, roll one-quarter inch thick and line a deep dish, leaving an inch over the sides to turn up over top crust; put in chicken, pour over gravy, cover with the other crust, with a large hole in center for steam to escape. Wet the edge and fold over the under crust, press firmly together; spread soft butter over the top, make ornament to fit the center and bake until done.

Chicken in Jelly. Boil a chicken or chickens in as little water as possible until the meat falls from the bones; pick off the meat, cut it rather fine, and season well with pepper and salt; put into the bottom and sides of a mould slices of hard-boiled eggs and fill nearly full with chicken. Boil down the broth till there is about a cupful left; season it well and pour over the chicken. It will form a jelly around the chicken. Let it stand on the ice over night or all day. To be sliced at table; garnish with fringed celery. If there is fear of the jelly not being stiff enough a little gelatine may be soaked and added.

Chicken Croquettes. One pound cooked chicken chopped fine, one-fourth pound white bread, one-fourth pound butter, four eggs, three large teaspoons finely chopped parsley, pinch of mace and nutmeg, one teapoon salt, one pinch cayenne pepper; pour enough boiling water over the bread to soften it, place on the fire with the yolks of two eggs and cook until smooth; set away to cool, while mixing the chicken with the rest of the eggs unbeaten, two tablespoons thick cream, the butter and seasoning; beat all thoroughly together till nicely mixed; let the mixture get quite cold before forming into croquettes. A famous Southern receipt.

Maryland Chicken. Singe, remove fine feathers, cut into pieces for serving, wipe, season with salt and pepper, dip in egg, roll in fine cracker crumbs; put pieces into a buttered dish and bake one hour, basting very often with one-third cup butter and one cup water. Serve with cream sauce.

Pressed Chicken. Boil chicken very tender; be sure to have plenty of liquor; separate white meat from the dark; soak three slices of bread in the liquor for a few minutes, then chop it up with the dark meat. Put white meat in the bottom of the dish, pour a little liquor on, then put on a layer of dark meat, leave until it is cold, and it will turn out like jelly.

Roast Duck. After the duck is drawn, wipe the inside with a clean cloth and prepare dressing as follows: One cup pounded cracker, moisten with hot milk or water, three medium sized onions, parboil and chop fine, little butter, sage, pepper and salt to taste; mix all together and fill the crop and body of the duck, leaving room for the dressing to swell; reserve the liver, gizzard and heart for gravy; tie the body of the duck firmly with a string (which is buttered to keep from burning), and put in the oven. Baste first with salt and water, and then with its own gravy, dredging them last with a little flour.

Potted Pigeons. Make dressing the same as for turkey, stuff them and fry in pork fat until nicely browned; take them out, pour the fat into a kettle with little water, put them into this, and let them simmer half an hour or more. When done, take them out, thicken the broth a little and pour over them.

Turkey. For a ten pound turkey take two pints bread crumbs, half teacup butter, cut in small pieces, one teaspoon summer savory, pepper and salt; fill turkey with little of the dressing, few strained oysters, alternating until filled. Put the oyster liquid in the pan with a pint of water; bake in a moderate oven.

EGGS.

"From the egg to the apples (for a dinner) from the beginning to the end."

Egg Vermicelli. Boil three eggs twenty minutes; separate the yolks and break the whites with a silver fork into fine pieces; toast four slices of bread, cut half into small squares and half into points or triangles; make one cup of thin, white sauce with one cup cream or milk, one teaspoon butter, one heaping teaspoon flour, one-half teaspoon salt, one-half saltspoon of pepper; stir the whites into the sauce, and when hot pour it over the squares of toast; rub the yolks through a fine strainer over the whole, and garnish with the toast points and parsley.

Omelette. 1. Soak one-half cup bread crumbs in a cup of milk, with salt to taste; when soft, add four well beaten eggs, and pour into a hot spider, in which is a generous piece of butter; cook slowly for ten minutes, slip a knife around the edges, roll or fold it and put on a platter.

2. Six eggs, whites beaten to a stiff froth, yolks well beaten; one cup warm milk, one tablespoon flour wet to a paste with cold milk; one teaspoon salt; mix all except the whites, add them last; cook immediately in a buttered spider for about ten minutes, fold like a turnover.

Baked Eggs. One pint milk, four eggs beaten separately, scald the milk and thicken with one tablespoon flour, let it cool a little; add the yolks, the whites, and a bit of salt; pour in a buttered dish and bake till it rises like a custard.

Shirred Eggs. Take as many eggs as there are persons to eat them; separate the eggs and beat whites to a stiff froth, drop it in a Washington pie tin in bunches, put yolk on top of each and a little pepper, salt and butter. Put in a very hot oven and brown lightly.

A La Cream. Boil ten eggs until hard; slice in rings; in the bottom of a baking dish place a layer of bread crumbs, then one of eggs; cover with bits of butter, pepper and salt, until all are used; pour over them a cup cream and brown in the oven.

Dropped. Drop fresh eggs into a saucepan of boiling water, with salt in it; have ready slices of buttered toast; then take up with a skimmer and lay on the toast.

VEGETABLES.

*"Earth's increase, foison plenty,
Barns and garners never empty,
Vines with clustering bunches growing,
Plants with goodly burthen bowing."*

TIME FOR COOKING VEGETABLES.

	SUMMER.	WINTER.
Green Peas,	1-2 hour	......
String Beans,	2 hours	......
Squash,	1 hour	1 hour
Asparagus,	1-2 hour	......
Cabbage,	1 hour	3 hours
Turnips,	1 hour	2 hours
Parsnips,	......	1 hour
Carrots,	......	1 1-2 hours
Beets,	1 hour	3 1-2 hours
Shelled Beans,	1 hour	......
Onions,	......	1 hour
Potatoes,	1-2 hour	1-2 hour
Potatoes, Baked,	......	1 hour
Spinage,	1 hour	1 1-2 hours
Corn,	1-2 hour	......
Sweet Potatoes,	......	3-4 hour
Sweet Potatoes, Baked,	......	1 hour

SALADS.

"To make a perfect salad there should be a miser for oil, a spendthrift for vinegar, a wise man for salt, and a madcap to stir the ingredients up and mix them well together."—[SPANISH PROVERB.]

Cabbage. Chop the cabbage, taking out the core and coarse parts of the leaves. Sprinkle with salt, black pepper, dry mustard and celery—salt to suit your taste. Two good sized cabbages, beat two eggs light, add two cups vinegar, piece butter the size of an egg, heat it until it comes to a boiling heat and thicken a little, stirring carefully all the time, and then pour it hot over the cabbage, mixing thoroughly. When cold it is fit to eat. Most excellent.

Chicken or Lobster. The meat of two lobsters or two chickens, three-quarters the same bulk of celery, yolks of five eggs, two teaspoons mustard, one teaspoon pepper, half teaspoon salt for lobster, whole teaspoon salt for chicken, one-third cup vinegar. One small bottle sweet oil stirred gradually into the egg, a few drops at a time. After it begins to thicken, add the other ingredients well mixed in the vinegar.

Egg. Boil a dozen eggs twenty minutes; cut them at one side and slip out the yolks; mash yolks smooth with small piece of butter, salt, a little made mustard; moisten with vinegar and salad oil alternately. Fill the whites with the mixture and serve on a lettuce leaf.

Salmon. One pint salmon, free from bones, skin and oil. Two parts white cabbage shredded fine, or cut; moisten with boiled dressing, garnish with dark green lettuce.

Dressing for Cabbage. One or two eggs, beaten, half teacup vinegar, one tablespoon mustard, butter half the size of an egg; thin with milk or cream—if milk, more butter should be used—teaspoon salt, two teaspoons sugar, pepper. Pour over chopped cabbage.

Dressing for Salad. Five tablespoons oil, half pint strong vinegar, two teaspoons mustard, one teaspoon salt, half teaspoon pepper, add little cayenne to taste, four eggs well beaten. Put vinegar on the stove in kettle of hot water and let it come to a scald, add the rest of ingredients and stir till it thickens.

Dressing for Lobster Salad. Four eggs, one teaspoon pepper, one teaspoon salt, two teaspoons mustard, five tablespoons butter. Beat all together until it thickens up smooth.

Leontine's Lobster. Two medium sized lobsters, one cup vinegar, piece butter size of an egg, put them on to boil. Beat up one or two eggs, one, teaspoon each salt, sugar, mustard, curry, half teaspoon pepper, juice of a lemon; put the mixture into the vinegar and cook until it thickens, adding rather more than half cup milk. Add lettuce or celery if desired. Very nice.

Salad Dressing. 1. Yolks of six eggs, one teaspoon mustard, one teaspoon salt, one teaspoon pepper, one and a half teaspoons sweet oil stirred gradually into the egg, few drops at a time, until perfectly smooth, then add half cup vinegar. Reserve little of the dressing without the vinegar, to which add capers and olives split.

2. One tablespoon mustard, one tablespoon butter or oil; rub mustard and oil together thoroughly and add one tablespoon salt, one tablespoon sugar, three eggs (well beaten), one cup rich milk; let the mixture warm slightly and add one cup strong vinegar; let it come almost to a boil; if bottled it will keep some time. Excellent with fish.

3. One and one-half cups cream, one-half or two-thirds cup vinegar, three eggs, one tablespoon mustard, one tablespoon oil or butter, one scant tablespoon salt, three tablespoons sugar; mix oil with mustard; add eggs, then salt and sugar; mix thoroughly with the vinegar and strain through coarse sieve; have the cream hot in milk boiler; add above mixture slowly, stir until it thickens. Milk and more butter can be used in place of cream.

4. **Bangor.** Two (rounded) tablespoons butter, two (scant) tablespoons flour; butter and flour cooked together till smooth; add slowly one cup (or less) of vinegar, two whole eggs or three yolks, two tablespoons sugar, dash of cayenne, one teaspoon mustard, stir into one pint hot milk; cook like soft custard; adding salt if needed; beat with egg beater and strain. One cup cream, whipped, is an improvement.

5. **Cream Dressing.** The yolks of two hard-boiled eggs rubbed very smoothly, then add dessertspoon mixed mustard, blend the two thoroughly, then stir in a tablespoon melted butter, half cup thick cream, little salt, cayenne pepper and sugar; add little by little vinegar enough to make the whole a smooth creamy mass. Last of all add the whites of two eggs, well beaten.

Mustard Dressing. Three tablespoons mustard, one and one-half teaspoons sugar, three-quarters teaspoon salt, enough boiling water to mix it; when cool add one and one-half tablespoons oil, and vinegar to thin it.

Yolks of eight eggs, well beaten, one-fourth cup sugar, one tablespoon salt, three tablespoons of the mustard described above, cayenne to taste, one-half cup milk, one cup butter; stir all together over the fire as you would soft custard. When somewhat cooled add one-half pint vinegar. Bottle tight.

Welsh Rare-bit. One-quarter pound nice cheese, cut in thin slices, put in a spider pouring over it a large cup milk, stirring until the cheese is dissolved, one-quarter teaspoon dry mustard, dash of pepper, and a pinch of salt; stir the mixture all the time till dissolved, add three pounded crackers, and a piece butter size of a butternut. As soon as they are stirred in turn into a warm dish and serve. Nice for tea.

PIES.

"Will't please you taste of what is here?"
—[Tempest.

Pie Crust. One quart flour, one-half pound lard, one-quarter pound butter, with water; knead till smooth, roll it out thin three times, touching it each time with the lard, sprinkling with flour and rolling it up to be rolled out again.

Pie Crust Glaze. To prevent juice soaking through a pie and making it soggy, wet the crust with the beaten white of an egg, before you put in the pie mixture. If the top of the pie is also wet it gives it a beautiful brown. Milk can be used on the top of a pie, and will be quite as satisfactory.

Cocoanut. Three cups flour, two of sugar, one of milk, one-half cup butter, flour, four eggs, two teaspoons cream tartar, one teaspoon soda, vanilla to flavor. FOR THE INSIDE: Whites two eggs, two cups powdered sugar; flavor with vanilla. Cover the first sheet of cake with a layer of this, then one of grated cocoanut; cover the top of the cake in the same way.

Cream. One cup sugar, heaping cup flour, three eggs, butter size of an egg, one teaspoon cream tartar, one-half teaspoon soda dissolved in a little hot water added just before going into the oven. CREAM: One cup milk, two eggs, two tablespoons flour, one-half cup sugar. Flavor with lemon.

Chess. Beat the yolks of three eggs till smooth, add one-half cup sugar and beat again, then add one-third cup butter, rubbed to a cream, and one-half teaspoon vanilla; bake on a plate lined with puff paste; when done, cover with the whites of three eggs, beaten stiff, and mixed with one-half cup powdered sugar and one teaspoon lemon juice. Brown slightly and cut while hot. Not to be served cold.

Lemon. 1. Six lemons, four cups sugar, six eggs, two ounces butter; grate the rind of the lemons and strain the juice; rub the butter and sugar together, then add the eggs well beaten, then the lemon. This makes two pies. Line the plates with rich puff paste and bake without top crust.

2. Juice and grated rind of one lemon, one cup sugar, one cup water, four eggs well beaten, (reserving the whites of two for frosting); cover plate with puff paste and bake without top crust. Beat reserved whites with two tablespoons sugar and put on top of pie and brown lightly.

3. Beat one cup sugar and one egg together, add juice and grated rind of one lemon, then one and one-half cups pounded cracker; bake on plate covered with rich paste; when done cover with whites of one egg and one-half cup sugar beaten together. Brown lightly.

4. **Extra.** Six apples, four lemons, four cups sugar, four eggs. Grate the lemons and apples.

Marlborough. 1. Two pounds apples, stewed and sifted, one pound butter, melted, one pound sugar, twelve eggs, juice of two lemons, five tablespoons cream, little nutmeg and cinnamon. Bake in rich puff paste. This amount makes five pies in medium-size plates.

2 Steam and strain six good sized apples, add while hot one tablespoon butter; when cool, stir in the yolks of three eggs, the grated rind and juice of one lemon,

one cup sugar. Bake on plates lined with puff paste and use the whites of the eggs for frosting.

Squash. 1. (Very Nice.) Peel, core, steam and strain one squash; thin with milk to the consistency of thick apple sauce; allow four eggs to one quart of milk. Beat the eggs, and add sugar, salt and lemon to taste.

2. One cup stewed and sifted squash, one cup boiling milk; when cool add one heaping cup sugar, two eggs, little salt, little nutmeg and cinnamon. The grated rind of a lemon is an improvement.

Orange. Juice and grated rind of one orange, one cup sugar, yolks of three eggs, one tablespoon corn starch stirred smooth with milk, one cup milk and piece butter size of a chestnut. Bake on plates lined with puff paste. Beat the whites of the eggs with three tablespoons sugar and put on top and brown

Mince Meat. Three pounds beef, one pound suet, one pound pork, cooked and chopped fine, add enough water from the meat to make moist; chop and add nine apples, three pounds raisins, and one pound citron; if currants are liked add one pound; then add one quart cider, one pint boiled cider, (wine or brandy may be used instead), four pounds brown sugar, two tablespoons cinnamon, two of nutmeg, one of mace, allspice and cloves; use salt to taste. The grated rind of lemon is an improvement.

Mock Mince. One cup sugar, one-half cup butter, one cup vinegar or wine, one-half cup molasses, one cup cold water, one cup raisins, one cup currants, three pounded crackers, two eggs, one lemon, salt, and teaspoon each of spice of all kinds. This quantity makes three pies.

Rhubarb. One cup chopped rhubarb, one cracker pounded fine, yolks of two eggs, one cup sugar, one teaspoon lemon, salt, and bits of butter. Whip the whites of the eggs for frosting.

Modern Rhubarb. One cup chopped rhubarb, one cup sugar, one egg.

Saratoga. One and one-half cups stewed apples, three eggs, one gill cream, one tablespoon butter, two of chopped citron, eight macaroons; melt the butter and mix thoroughly with the other ingredients and bake between two crusts.

Apple Custard. One quart stewed and sifted apple, one quart milk, one cup sugar, two tablespoons melted butter, little grated lemon and nutmeg, six eggs, well beaten. Bake without top crust.

Bambury Tart. One coffee cup raisins, seeded, and chopped fine, one cup sugar, one egg, juice and grated rind of one lemon; stir all into a paste. Make a puff paste and cut into rounds with a biscuit cutter; place a teaspoon of prepared mixture on a round, and cover with another round, pressing the edges well together. Bake in a quick oven. Fine for picnics.

Cream Raspbeary. Line a pie dish with puff paste and fill with well sweetened raspberries; cover with a crust but do not pinch down the edges; butter the lower edge to prevent adhesion; bake in a quick oven. While this is cooking, heat a small cup of milk, add a pinch of soda, then stir in one teaspoon corn starch, wet in cold milk, and one teaspoon sugar and cook three minutes. Remove from stove and beat in the frothed whites of two eggs; beat until it is a stiff cream, and when cold raise the top crust of the pie and pour the cream mixture over the raspberries, then replace the crust and let it get cold before serving.

PUDDINGS.

"The daintiest last, to make the end more sweet."
[—King Richard II.

Apple. One quart flour, one pint milk, one teaspoon soda, two teaspoons cream tartar, and small piece butter; roll out and fill with sliced apples; steam three hours. Served with sauce.

Apple Charlotte. Butter an earthen dish, and place around the sides slices of bread which have been cut about one inch thick, then soak in cold water and spread with butter, fill dish with sliced apple, grate over them one nutmeg, add one cup sugar, one cup water; cover with slices of bread which have been soaked and buttered and place a large plate over the dish and bake four hours; remove from the oven and let it get cool. When ready to serve, loosen around the edges with a knife and turn out on a dish. Serve with sugar and cream.

Apple Cream. Three tart apples, baked slowly (be careful not to brown the pulp); remove the skin and cores and strain, add one and one-half cups sugar, whites of two eggs, beaten stiff, and juice of one lemon; beat to a stiff froth. Serve with boiled custard made of the yolks of the eggs.

Charlotte Russe. One-third box gelatine dissolved in a coffee cup milk, one pint cream, sweetened and flavored with vanilla; beat together and let it stand until it begins to stiffen, then stir in the beaten whites of five eggs; line a dish with thin slices of plain cake (sponge being best), and pour in the mixture and set away to harden. When ready to serve, turn out on a dish.

Chocolate. Boil two cups bread crumbs in one quart milk till it thickens then let it cool; beat the yolks of five and the whites of two eggs with one cup sugar and three tablespoons grated chocolate, and add to the cooled mixture and bake one-half hour; beat the whites of three eggs with five tablespoons sugar and a small teaspoon vanilla, and spread over the pudding when cold and brown lightly. Eat cold with or without cream.

College. Yolks of two eggs, one-half cup sugar, one-half cup butter, one cup milk, one pint flour, teaspoon cream tartar, one-half teaspoon soda. SAUCE: Whites of two eggs, one and one-half cups sugar and juice of one lemon beaten stiff.

Cottage. One cup sugar, one egg, three tablespoons melted butter, one cup milk, two cups flour, one teaspoon cream tartar, one-half teaspoon soda. Bake one-half hour. Serve with hot sauce.

Cracker. One quart milk, eight tablespoons pounded cracker, four tablespoons sugar, five eggs, one-half pound raisins, piece of butter on top. Bake one-half hour.

Columbia. Two and one-half cups flour, one cup molasses, one cup sour milk, one-half teaspoon cinnamon, one teaspoon soda, one-half cup chopped pork or suet, one-half cup raisins. Steam three hours.

Cocoanut. Boil ten minutes one quart milk and three tablespoons tapioca (which has soaked in water over night), then add and let boil five minutes longer, the beaten yolks of four eggs, one cup sugar, three tablespoons cocoanut; this should be cooking enough; pour in a fancy dish and cover with the whites of the eggs, beaten to a stiff froth with three tablespoons sugar; sprinkle cocoanut on top and brown lightly. To be eaten cold.

Indian. 1. One quart milk (reserving one cup); scald the milk, add three tablespoons meal wet in a little cold milk; boil two minutes, then add one cup molasses, the remainder of the milk, one-half cup cold water, one egg. Bake in a moderate oven at least three hours.

2. Three tablespoons Indian meal, one cup molasses, two quarts milk, two eggs, butter half the size of an egg, one tablespoon ginger and two teaspoons salt. Boil half the milk and pour it on the meal, then add all the rest and bake four or five hours.

English Plum. Two cups molasses, one cup milk, two cups chopped suet, two cups chopped raisins, one teaspoon salt, two teaspoons soda, beat in the molasses, nutmeg, cloves and mace to taste, few strips citron and flour enough to make it stiff. Steam five hours.

2. Beat six yolks and four whites of eggs very light, and add to them a tumbler of sweet milk; stir in gradually one-fourth pound grated stale bread, one pound flour, three-quarters pound sugar, pound each of beef suet, chopped fine, currants nicely washed and dried, stoned raisins well floured; stir well, then add two nutmegs, a tablespoon mace, one of cinnamon, one-half of cloves, one wine glass brandy, one tea-

spoon salt, and finally another tumbler of milk; one pound of citron (blanched sweet almonds are also a great addition but may be omitted); boil in bowls or moulds five hours. These will keep for months. When wanted steam one hour. Serve with a sauce made of drawn butter, sugar, wine and nutmeg.

Mountain Dew. One pint milk, four tablespoons pounded cracker, yolks three eggs well beaten; bake to a light brown; beat the whites of the eggs with one cup sugar and the juice of one lemon, spread over the pudding and brown lightly. To be eaten cold.

Queen of Puddings. One pint bread crumbs, one quart milk, yolks four eggs, piece butter size of an egg, one cup sugar, the grated rind of one lemon; bake one-half hour. Spread preserves or jelly on top, then cover with the whites of the eggs, beaten to a stiff froth with one cup sugar and the juice of one lemon. Brown lightly.

Scarboro Puffs. One quart milk, one tablespoon butter, twelve eggs, little salt; boil the milk, and while boiling, stir in flour until the batter is stiff enough for the spoon to stand up in when cold; after it is cold, stir in the butter, and one egg at a time without beating; drop from a spoon into hot lard and fry a light brown; roll while hot in sugar and cinnamon, mixed. SAUCE: To a cup of cream, beaten to a froth, add one cup sugar and flavor to taste.

Sponge. One cup sugar, one-half cup butter, one cup milk, four eggs, two teaspoons cream tartar, one of soda, three cups flour. Bake one hour. Eat with liquid sauce.

Tapioca Cream. Soak over night three tablespoons tapioca in water enough to soften and cover it; in the morning scald one quart milk and stir in the tapioca, then add the yolks of three eggs, well beaten with one cup sugar and a little salt. Beat the whites of the eggs with three tablespoons sugar and spread on top. To be eaten cold.

Orange Cream. Soak one-fourth box gelatine in one-fourth cup cold water till well softened; scald one pint milk and pour over the gelatine, and stir in the yolks of two eggs and sugar to taste; when smooth and thick, strain and cool, then add the juice of three or four oranges and a little orange flavoring, and the stiffly beaten whites of the eggs, or better still, one cup whipped cream. Set on ice until wanted.

Rye. One pint milk, two eggs, little salt, three tablespoons rye meal; steam one-half hour, and then the rye should be on top and bottom with the custard between. Serve with sauce.

Pineapple. Soak one-half box gelatine in one-half cup water two hours; grate one small pineapple into a sauce pan with one cup sugar, one cup water, simmer ten minutes, add the gelatine and strain; when cool, add the whites of four eggs, and beat until it begins to thicken, then put into a mould to harden. Serve cold with a soft custard flavored with wine.

Carrot. One-half pint grated bread crumbs, one-fourth pound flour, one-fourth pound butter, one-half pound candied cherries, one-half pound boiled and sifted carrot, one-half pound sugar, one teaspoon baking powder, little salt and two eggs. Steam in melon mould two and one-half hours. Serve with hot sauce.

PUDDINGS.

Apple Meringue. Make a syrup of one and one-half pints water, two cups sugar and one lemon; pare and quarter ten apples, cook in the syrup until they are red, then put in a dish that will hold at least one quart; make a custard of one pint milk, yolks three eggs, one-half cup sugar and flavor with lemon; when it becomes cold, pour over the apples and cover with frosting made from the whites of the eggs and two tablespoons confectioners' sugar. Brown in the oven. To be eaten cold.

Fig. One-half pound bread crumbs, one-half pound figs chopped fine, one-half pound suet, chopped fine, little salt, one-half cup sugar, two eggs well beaten; flavor with nutmeg. Boil in a tin pudding mould four hours. Eat with hot sauce

Almond Rice. Blanch one-half cup almonds; put with one cup well washed rice, one-fourth cup sugar, one-half teaspoon salt, into three cups hot milk and cook in double boiler till the rice is tender. Serve hot or cold with jelly and whipped cream.

Snow Balls. One cup flour, three well beaten eggs, one cup sugar, one tablespoon milk, one-half teaspoon soda, one teaspoon cream tartar. Steam in cups thirty minutes. Serve with liquid sauce.

Prune Whip. Soak one pound prunes over night; in the morning stew till tender with one cup sugar, then rub through a sieve; beat till stiff the whites of four eggs, then add the sifted prunes and the grated rind and juice of one lemon; beat all well together, then heap on a dish and bake in the oven till a delicate brown. Serve with whipped cream or a custard made with one pint milk, the beaten yolks four eggs, four tablespoonssugar and a little salt. Flavor with vanilla. To be eaten cold.

Coburg. Heat three cups milk in a double boiler; cook one-half cup well washed rice in one cup boiling water five minutes, or till the water is absorbed, then turn it into the hot milk and cook till tender; add one teaspoon salt, one teaspoon butter, one well beaten egg, two tablespoons sugar, and let it cook a few minutes; turn into a dish for serving, and sift over the top a little sugar and cinnamon, and dot thickly with butter. Set it in the oven a few minutes when ready to serve.

Caramel Custard. One-half cup sugar, put in a pan and stir till it melts and is brown, then add two teaspoons water and one quart hot milk; beat six eggs with a little salt, one teaspoon vanilla, stir into the milk and pour into a buttered mould; set the mould in a pan of hot water and bake thirty minutes. Serve cold with a sauce made with one-half cup sugar, put in a pan and melted, and when brown, add one-half cup water and boil ten minutes. It can be flavored with vanilla or not.

Lemon Jelly. One-half box gelatine, soaked till soft in cup water; take one pint water and boil an inch piece of stick cinnamon, and the grated rind of two lemons, ten minutes, then add the gelatine, one cup sugar, one-half cup lemon juice, and when well dissolved, strain and set on ice.

Tipsy Trifle. Take six oranges, remove skin, white part and seeds; slice, put in dish with cup sugar sprinkled over them and let stand two hours. For the cream: one quart milk, yolks five eggs, one-half cup sugar, one-half cup flour, little salt; scald milk, add eggs, sugar and flour; stir briskly; add one teaspoon vanilla, grated rind two oranges; place oranges in dish and cover with cream. Beat whites of eggs to a stiff froth; add two cups powdered sugar, one-quarter teaspoon cream tartar, little vanilla, beat until stiff. Take one-half and color with strawberry, then put in dish spoonful each alternately; brown in oven. To be eaten cold. This is delicious as well as ornamental.

Strawberry Trifle. One cup sugar, one-half cup milk, two eggs, two cups flour, one teaspoon cream tartar, one-half teaspoon soda. Bake this in Washington pie tins. It will make two.

For filling, take one cup milk, yolk of one egg, one tablespoon flour, two tablespoons sugar and cook. Just before serving, split the cakes and fill with mashed strawberries and put the custard on top. Beat the whites of two eggs and put on top of the custard and dot with berries.

Fruit. Dissolve one box gelatine in one pint cold water, then add one pint boiling water, two cups sugar and the juice of three lemons; strain and let it stand till it begins to harden, then add two oranges, cut in small pieces, two sliced bananas, six figs cut fine (if you like them), six dates cut fine, ten chopped nuts, one-half pound candied cherries, and one-quarter pound of angelica. Any kind of candied fruit can be used as well as those named. Wine can be added. Serve with whipped cream.

Fruit Salad. Bananas and oranges sliced and mixed in a salad bowl; to the juice of two oranges add one gill sherry wine, two ounces sugar, the white of one egg. Simmer this for five minutes, but do not let it boil, then strain, and when cool, pour over the fruit and place it on ice till time to serve.

SAUCES.

"Hunger is the best sauce."

1. Beat one-half cup butter to a cream, then add one cup powdered sugar, four tablespoons wine or brandy, and one-quarter cup cream. Place bowl in hot water and stir over the fire till creamy.

2. One tablespoon flour rubbed with one-half cup butter, one cup sugar. Stir into one cup boiling milk and add one egg beaten separately.

3. One cup butter, one cup sugar, creamed together, with one box of strawberries or raspberries; makes a delicious sauce for cottage or bread puddings.

Hard Sauce. Rub one cup sugar, one-half cup butter to a cream, then add the beaten white of one egg and put on ice to harden.

Mollie's Pudding. Stir one egg, one cup sugar till foamy and the sugar is dissolved. Cook one dessertspoon flour in three tablespoons of water ten minutes, beat into the sugar one egg just before serving. Flavor with vanilla.

Plain Pudding. Melt one heaping tablespoon butter, add two tablespoons flour, stir in one and one-half cups hot water, cook well, then add one and one-half cups sugar, two teaspoons lemon juice and a little nutmeg.

Raspberry Foam. One cup mashed raspberries, one cup sugar and white of one egg. Use strawberries if you like.

Wine. Wet one tablespoon corn starch in cold water, stir in one cup boiling water; cook ten minutes. Rub one-fourth cup butter with one cup sugar, then add one well beaten egg, one saltspoon grated nutmeg and one-half cup wine, and add to the hot corn starch, stirring until well mixed.

For Whipped Cream. One tablespoon gelatine, dissolved and flavored, can be stirred into cream, and will give a little more body to it.

Foaming Sauce. Beat one-half cup butter to a cream, add one cup granulated sugar and stir until it is white and foaming. Just before serving, pour on it one cup boiling water and stir a moment.

FROZEN DISHES.

"That makes one's mouth water."

Arrowroot Ice. One large tablespoon arrowroot, mixed with cold water; pour upon it very slowly one quart boiling water, the juice of four lemons, a little of the peel shred very fine, with one pound of sugar. Stir it together and freeze.

Bisque Glace. Two quarts cream, one-half dozen macaroons, pounded fine (they must be stale if not dried in the stove), pour a little cream over them and allow them to stand till they soften. Beat until very fine then add the rest of the cream and freeze. It is not well to have the macaroons too thick in the cream.

Cafe Parfait. Line a mould with coffee ice cream, made with one pint milk, one egg, one scant tablespoon flour, one-half teaspoon salt, one cup sugar, one-half cup coffee, one pint cream, and freeze; then into this lining of cream put a whipped cream mixture of one pint cream, one cup sugar, one-half cup strong coffee chilled and whipped. Pack the mould in ice and salt, let stand two hours before serving.

Caramel, for coloring ice creams, soups, jellies and sauces. Melt one cup sugar (brown or white) with one tablespoon of water in a frying pan; stir until it becomes a dark brown color; add one cup boiling water;

simmer ten minutes and bottle when cool; this should be kept on hand, as it is useful for many purposes; it gives a rich dark color to soups, coffee and jelly, and is a delicious flavoring in ice cream, custards and pudding sauces.

Chocolate Cream. Scrape one-fourth pound chocolate very fine, put it in a quart of rich milk or cream; boil it until dissolved stirring occasionally; thicken with one egg. When cream is used the egg may be dispensed with. Then freeze.

Coffee Cream. One-half cup boiled coffee, one-half cup sugar, yolks of two eggs; when cool add one pint whipped cream, sweetened with one-half cup sugar; stir all well; put in ice cream freezer and pack like ice cream. Do not turn crank. Freeze from four to five hours.

Frozen Pudding. One pint milk, one pint cream, one tablespoon gelatine, one egg, one heaping cup sugar, one cup figs, one cup raisins, one cup dates; soak gelatine in a little of the milk about twenty minutes; scald the rest of the milk and cream, and when hot pour onto the beaten egg and sugar, and then pour the whole on the gelatine and stir until dissolved, then add the fruit. Cool and freeze.

Ice Cream. Five eggs, one pint milk, two cups sugar, little salt. Make custard of above over night. In the morning add three pints cold milk, one cup sugar, two tablespoons vanilla flavoring.

Delicious Ice Cream. One quart cream, one pint milk, three cups sugar, three tablespoons ground coffee; whip the cream until it is of a velvetry consistency and will pour; put sugar and milk into freezer, stir to dissolve, then add the cream, whipped a little at a time; steep the coffee ten minutes in two-thirds cup of boiling water, strain through a cloth. When cold add to the mixture and freeze. If vanilla is used one tablespoon is enough.

Ice Cream. One quart milk, six or eight eggs, one cup sugar, one pint to one quart cream. Sugar to taste. Flavor to taste. Make a boiled custard with the milk, sugar and the yolks of the eggs; cook it slightly but not curdled; strain, and when cool, add the cream and sugar to make it quite sweet, and any flavoring desired. If cream can not be obtained beat the whites of the eggs till foamy and add them just before freezing. Use one-fourth box gelatine for two quarts of custard; soak in one-half cup cold milk and dissolve in the boiling custard when taken from the fire. If the custard should curdle it will become smooth when frozen. Very nice.

Fruit Ice Cream. Two quarts milk, six eggs, about one and one-half pound sugar, one and a half tablespoons Bermuda arrowroot. Cook it as a custard. When cold flavor with two tablespoons vanilla and three wine glasses Sherry wine; then add one pound figs, one-quarter pound citron, and other fruits cut fine. Freeze like ice cream.

Strawberry Ice Cream. Sprinkle sugar over the berries; mash and rub through a fine sieve. Measure the juice and use one pint of juice to two quarts well sweetened cream.

Ice Cream. One quart cream, not too rich, one wine glass Sherry wine, one teacup white sugar. Mix thoroughly and freeze. Ripe strawberries or peaches cut up, well sweetened, and mixed with cream are very nice frozen.

FROZEN DISHES.

Lemon Ice. One quart water, juice six lemons, one pound sugar, one gill cream (scant one-half cup), two teaspoons lemon extract. Mix thoroughly, strain and freeze.

Lemon Sherbet 1. Two quarts cold water, two pounds sugar, boiled together twenty-five minutes, two tablespoons gelatine soaked in some of the water and sugar meanwhile. After the water and sugar are taken off add the gelatine, strained, and when the whole is quite cold put in juice of six lemons; add two or three eggs beaten to a froth when partly frozen.

2. One tablespoon gelatine, one quart water, one pint of sugar, juice six lemons. The boiling water used in dissolving the gelatine should be part of the quart of water.

3. One quart milk, one pint sugar, the grated rind of one lemon, boiled together; cool, and put into the freezer; when partly frozen add the juice of five lemons and the beaten whites of three eggs.

Orange Water Ice. Eight oranges, three lemons, three pounds loaf sugar, one box gelatine dissolved in cold water enough to make one and one-half gallons. Extract the oil of rind of oranges and lemons by rubbing the rind with lumps of sugar.

Velvet Cream. Six eggs, two coffee cups granulated sugar; beat eggs and sugar together until very light; add two quarts of milk, one quart hot and one quart cold; put the cold milk over the eggs and sugar, stir well, then add the hot milk; put into milk boiler, stir constantly ten minutes till it becomes very thick. When cool flavor with vanilla, then freeze. This can be improved by adding cream--to every pint of cream add one-half teacup sugar.

Walnut Bisque. One quart cream, one cup sugar, scalded together. To this add one square of chocolate, melted; strain and add one tablespoon vanilla, one cup English walnuts, broken. Then freeze.

Water Ice. One tumbler any kind of preserved fruit, raspberries, pineapple or currants are the best, because they have more flavor. Strain it through a sieve, pouring over it as you strain it three pints of water sweetened to taste, and freeze hard and solid, or it is not good. If the preserve has not flavor enough grated lemon peel or the peel of a Mandarin orange will make it good. Brandy peaches are extremely good, and the wild grape is very nice as it has such a beautiful color. Jelly is just as good as preserve in freezing. No gelatine, white of egg or arrowroot is needed.

CAKE.

"Where honey is, there are the bees."

"Three rounding teaspoons baking powder are equal to one level teaspoon of soda and two full teaspoons of cream tartar."—*Mrs. Lincoln.*

Almond. 1. One and a half cups sugar, half cup butter, two-thirds cup milk, three cups flour, whites of seven eggs, one teaspoon cream tartar, one-half teaspoon soda, small cup almonds blanched and pounded, one large teaspoon of almond essence. Flavor frosting with rose water.

2. One cup butter, two cups sugar, three and one-half cups flour, one-half cup milk, whites eight eggs, two teaspoons cream tartar, one teaspoon soda. Flavor with almond.

3. Two cups sugar, one cup butter, whites six eggs, one cup milk, three and a half cups flour, heaping teaspoon cream tartar, half teaspoon soda, three teaspoons almond extract, half pound blanched almonds on top. Sprinkle with sugar.

Almond Silver. One coffee cup sugar, one-half cup butter, beaten together to a cream; one-half cup milk, one-half teaspoon cream tartar, one-quarter teaspoon soda. Add whites four eggs, beaten to a stiff froth, and two full cups flour. Flavor with almond.

Almond or White. Whites of six eggs, two cups sugar, one cup butter, one cup milk, three cups flour, one teaspoon cream tartar, half teaspoon soda dissolved in the milk, two teaspoons almond essence.

Angel. Whites of eleven eggs, one and one-half cups granulated sugar, one cupful flour, measured after being sifted four times, one teaspoon cream tartar, one teaspoon vanilla extract; sift the flour and cream tartar together; beat the whites to a stiff froth; beat the sugar slowly into the eggs, adding the seasoning and flour, stirring quickly and lightly; bake for forty minutes in a moderate oven. Do not grease the pan, and use a new tin or a bright one.

Blueberry. One-half cup butter creamed, one cup sugar, two eggs, one cup milk, one teaspoon soda, two teaspoons cream tartar in one and one-half pints of flour; little salt, roll one pint blueberries in two handfuls of flour.

Boston Gingerbread. One pound sugar, one pound butter, two pounds flour, six eggs, one pint molasses, one gill of water, one teaspoon soda, two teaspoons each allspice, cloves and mace, one quart of fruit, half pound of citron. Bake in two loaves three hours.

Boston Puffs. Half pint boiling milk, piece butter size of walnut, salt, one and a half cups flour scalded together. When cool, beat in three eggs separately. Fry in lard, as pancakes, then roll in sugar and cinnamon mixed.

Bread. Three cups of raised dough, two cups sugar, one-half cup butter, one cup raisins, teaspoon soda, spice to taste.

Bride's. 1. One-half cup butter, two cups sugar, whites five eggs, one cup cold water, three cups flour, one teaspoon soda, two of cream tartar, sift last two into the flour. Flavor with almond. Make one sheet.

2. Whites of four eggs, one cup sugar, half cup butter, one-half cup milk, two cups flour, two teaspoons cream tartar, half teaspoon soda. Flavor with almond.

Bridgewater. Two cups sugar, two-thirds cup butter, three eggs, three and a half cups flour, one cup sweet milk, half teaspoon soda, one teaspoon cream tartar.

Caramel. Two cups sugar, three-fourths cup butter, not quite a cup milk, whites of eight eggs, three cups flour, two teaspoons baking powder. Flavor to taste. Bake in three layers. ICING:—Two cups sugar, butter size of a walnut, not quite a cup of milk. Boil ten minutes, cool, then beat until stiff enough to spread on the cake.

Chocolate Cake. One cup butter, two cups sugar, three and a half cups flour, five eggs, leaving out whites of two, one cup milk, teaspoon cream tartar, one-half teaspoon soda. FROSTING:—While hot, frost with the following: Whites of two eggs, one and a half cups sugar, six tablespoons grated chocolate.

2. One cup sugar, half cup butter, two cups milk, two cups flour, two eggs, teaspoon soda; grate two squares chocolate, mix with another half cup milk, add yolk of one egg, one teaspoon vanilla and sweeten to taste. Boil the mixture until soft, add to the other, bake three-quarters of an hour.

3 One cup sugar, one-fourth cup butter, one-fourth cup milk, one-half cup grated chocolate, dissolved in one-fourth cup boiling water, two eggs, one cup bread

flour, one teaspoon cream tartar, one-half teaspoon soda. Flavor with vanilla and frost with boiled chocolate frosting.

Chocolate Cocoanut. One-half cup butter, one cup sugar, one egg and yolks of two, one cup sweet milk, two cups flour, one tablespoon baking powder, two small cakes of chocolate, one-fourth cup cocoanut, salt; beat sugar and butter together, add the beaten eggs, flour, powder and milk; put cocoanut in milk to soften and add melted chocolate last. Bake in three layers. Fill with one cup sugar, boil until it hairs; beat the whites of the two eggs to a stiff froth, add one-fourth cake chocolate, one-fourth cup cocoanut. Flavor with vanilla. Improves by keeping a little while.

Citron. One pound sugar, three-quarters pound butter, one pound flour, eight eggs, half cup sour milk, one-half teaspoon cream tartar, one teaspoon soda, one pound citron.

Clove. Two cups sugar, one cup butter, two cups stoned raisins, chopped fine, one teaspoon cloves, two of nutmeg, one and one-half of cinnamon, one cup milk, two eggs, one-half teaspoon soda, one teaspoon cream tartar, two and one-half cups flour. This cake is better when a week old than when first baked.

Cocoanut. 1. One cup sugar, two cups flour, two cups cocoanut, two tablespoons butter, two eggs, teaspoon cream tartar, half teaspoon soda. Soak the cocoanut in a cup of milk.

2. Two cups sugar, one cup butter, one cup milk, four cups flour, teaspoon soda, two of cream tartar, whites of seven eggs, one cup grated cocoanut. FROSTING:—Whites of three eggs, one cup grated cocoanut, sugar as for other frosting.

3. Four cups flour, three cups sugar, one cup butter, one cup milk, one teaspoon cream tartar, one-half teaspoon soda, five eggs, one cocoanut grated, juice of a lemon.

4. One pound sugar, one-half pound butter, three-quarters pound flour, five eggs, one cocoanut grated.

5. One cup butter, two cups sugar, whites of ten eggs, four cups flour, one cup milk, one cup prepared cocoanut soaked in the milk, two teaspoons baking powder. Bake in sheets in a rather quick oven. If you use the fresh cocoanut use two cups of it.

6. **One, Two, Three, Four.** One cup butter, two cups sugar, three cups flour, four eggs (using the whites only), one cup milk, one teaspoon cream tartar sifted into the flour, one-half teaspoon soda in the milk, one-half of a cocoanut, grated, and stirred in at the last.

Cocoanut Cream. Three eggs, one cup sugar, one cup flour, two tablespoons melted butter, three tablespoons milk, one teaspoon cream tartar, one-half teaspoon soda. FILLING:—One-half pint milk, one tablespoon flour, small pinch salt, three tablespoons sugar, yolk of one egg; the white for frosting. Use shredded cocoanut in both frosting and filling, and flavor with vanilla.

Cold Water. Two cups sugar, one cup butter, one cup cold water, four cups flour, one cup each raisins and currants, three eggs, teaspoon soda, half teaspoon cream tartar, salt, teaspoon each of all kinds spice. Put all together and stir well with the hand until smooth.

Composition. Two cups butter, three cups sugar, one cup milk, five cups flour, five eggs, one pound raisins, one nutmeg, teaspoon soda.

Cookies. One-half pound butter, one-half pound sugar, two eggs, reserving white of one egg, scant teaspoon soda; roll very thin, lay two or three blanched almonds on cake before baking. Wet soda in a drop of milk. Flour sufficient to roll. Rich.

2. One-half cup butter, one cup sugar, one-half cup milk, one egg, flour enough to roll.

3. One cup butter, two cups sugar, one-half cup sour cream, one-third cup milk, three eggs, one teaspoon soda, one teaspoon cream tartar. Nutmeg and lemon.

Cocoanut Cookies. Two cups sugar, one cup butter, two cups grated cocoanut, two eggs, one teaspoon baking powder. Mix with enough flour to roll very thin. Bake in quick oven but not brown.

Molasses Cookies. 1. One egg, one cup molasses, one-half cup butter, one even teaspoon soda; ginger to taste, little salt. Flour to roll thin.

2. To one cup of molasses boiled for a moment, add one-half cup shortening; let it melt in, then stir thoroughly; when partly cool stir in flour with one teaspoon soda sifted in it till it is as hard as possible, then set away to cool. After it is perfectly cold roll out as thin as possible and bake quickly. Put in salt and one teaspoon of ginger when mixing it.

Soft Molasses Cookies. One cup sugar, one cup molasses, one cup sour milk, three-fourths cup shortening, half of which shall be butter or lard; beef drippings may be used for the remainder; one heaping teaspoon soda, one egg not beaten, salt and ginger to taste; work shortening and sugar together, stir in egg, sift soda into flour; mix very stiff, roll out one-half inch thick and cut into rounds.

Rice Flour Cookies. One-half pound sugar, one-half pound rice flour, four eggs.

Sugar Cookies. Beat one cup butter to a cream, then add two cups sugar, two eggs, one tablespoon milk, four and one-half cups flour, one-half teaspoon soda mixed with it; roll thin; bake quick.

Corn Starch. One cup butter, two cups sugar, one cup sweet milk, one cup corn starch, two cups flour, whites of seven eggs, teaspoon soda, two teaspoons cream tartar; flavor with lemon or almond; frosting will improve it. Very nice.

Cream. Two cups sugar, one cup sour cream, rubbed together; two well beaten eggs. teaspoon saleratus dissolved in milk, flour enough to make it a little stiffer than common cake; flavor to taste; bake from half to three-quarters of an hour.

Cream Cakes. 1. One pint hot water, half pound butter, three-quarters pound flour, ten eggs, one teaspoon soda, dry; boil the water and butter together and stir in the flour while boiling; let it cool, then stir in the eggs one at a time, without beating. Drop on buttered tins and bake in a hot oven. INSIDE:— One cup flour, two cups sugar, one quart milk, four eggs, pinch of salt; boil the milk, beat the flour, sugar and eggs together, and stir into the milk while boiling. Flavor.

2. Let one cupful of hot water and one-half cupful of butter come to a boil; while boiling stir in one cup flour; when cold, stir in three eggs, not beaten. Drop by spoonfuls into a buttered tin and bake in a quick oven. FILLING:—One cup milk, one-half cup sugar, bring to a boil and add two tablespoons flour, or one tablespoon corn starch, beaten smooth, with a spoonful milk, one egg, well beaten. When the cream cakes are cold, split, but not wholly; lay round and fill.

Crullers. Three tablespoons sugar, three tablespoons lard, three eggs, mix like doughnuts; fry quick, turn every second.

Crumpets. One cup brown sugar, one cup chopped raisins, one-half cup butter, one egg, half teaspoon soda in a large spoon of milk; all kinds of spice; roll thin.

Currant. Three-quarters of a cup of butter, two cups sugar, three cups flour, one cup milk, one and one-half cups currants, four eggs, one teaspoon soda, two teaspoons cream tartar.

Dayton. One cup butter, two cups sugar, three cups flour, five eggs, one-half cup milk, teaspoon cream tartar, one-half teaspoon soda. This cake is very nice spiced a good deal, with raisins and other fruit added.

Delicate. 1. Two cups sugar, one-half cup butter, whites of six eggs, three-quarters cup sweet milk, nearly three cups flour, half teaspoon soda, one teaspoon cream tartar; lemon for flavoring.

2. One and one-half cups sugar, one-half cup butter, one-half cup milk, half teaspoon soda, two cups flour, into which rub one teaspoon cream tartar. Add last the whites of four eggs beaten to a stiff froth. Flavor with lemon.

Delicious. 1. Two cups sugar, one cup butter, one cup milk, three cups flour, three eggs, half teaspoon soda, scant teaspoon cream tartar; stir the butter and sugar together, add beaten yolks, then the beaten whites. Dissolve the soda in the milk, rub cream tartar in the flour and add the last thing. Very nice.

2. One pound sugar, one-half pound butter, yolks of fourteen eggs, one pound flour, two teaspoons cream tartar sifted in flour, one cup sweet cream, one teaspoon soda dissolved in a little water. Bake in a quick oven.

Doughnuts. 1. Two cups sugar, two cups sour milk, two eggs, small piece melted butter, teaspoon soda, little salt. Make very soft, better to stand a few days before frying.

2. Aunt Caroline's. Two quarts flour, two and a half cups granulated sugar, two eggs, two-thirds cup yeast mixed together; stir teaspoon of cinnamon, teaspoon salt, butter size of a large egg into two-thirds of a pint of milk heated. Mix the above ingredients with the milk. Rise over night; knead well.

3. Aunt Grant's. Six heaping tablespoons sugar, one of butter, two or three eggs, cup sour milk, half teaspoon soda, spice.

4. One pint sweet milk, one teaspoon soda, two cups sugar, one-half cup butter, four eggs, one nutmeg, salt, flour enough to roll out.

Molasses Drop. One cup sugar, one cup molasses, one-half cup butter or lard, one cup cold water, one egg, one large teaspoon soda, five cups flour. Flavor with cloves and cinnamon.

English Walnut. One scant cup butter, two cups sugar, three cups flour, one cup milk, four eggs, one pound English walnuts, one teaspoon cream tartar, half teaspoon soda. Bake in sheets.

Feather. One and a half cups sugar, three cups flour, one-quarter cup butter, three-quarters cup milk, two eggs, two teaspoons cream tartar, one teaspoon soda, salt, flavor with lemon.

Fig. Two cups sugar, one-half cup butter, one cup milk, whites five eggs, beaten stiff, three cups flour, two teaspoons baking powder; about one cup figs cut up quite fine and sifted over with flour. Soaking them over night in wine or brandy improves them. Nice.

Filling for a Layer Cake. Grate one large, tart apple, one lemon grated and the juice squeezed out, one egg, one cup sugar. Let this boil for five minutes; stir it constantly. Eat while fresh.

French. Two cups sugar, one-half cup butter, one cup milk, three cups flour, two teaspoons cream tartar, one teaspoon soda dissolved in milk. Beat the sugar, butter, cream tartar and yolks together, whites separately, four eggs.

French Loaf. One pound sugar, half pound butter, two eggs, half pint milk, one pound flour, one tea-spoon soda, one pound raisins, one cup currants, one nutmeg, citron, wine-glass of brandy.

Fruit. One pound citron, two pounds currants, two pounds raisins, one pound flour, one pound butter, one pound sugar, nine eggs, half teaspoon soda, half cup molasses, teaspoon each, cloves, nutmeg, mace, cinnamon and allspice, and two of lemon.

2. Five eggs, two cups brown sugar, one-half cup molasses, one and a half cups butter, three and a half cups flour, three-quarters pound citron, one and a half pounds currants, same of raisins, spice of all kinds. Bake three or four hours very slowly.

3. One and one-half pounds brown sugar, one pound butter (or two cups melted), one pound flour (or one quart), four pounds raisins chopped, three pounds

currants, one pound citron, chopped or sliced, one-half pound chopped almonds, ten eggs, three tablespoons cassia, three tablespoons cloves, two tablespoons mace, three nutmegs, two ounces vanilla or part rose extract, teaspoon soda dissolved in one-half cup coffee, brandy or butter. Add the beaten whites of the eggs the last thing. Steam four hours and dry in the oven for twenty minutes. It will keep perfectly for an indefinite time if not eaten.

German. One cup butter, two cups sugar, three and a half cups flour, half teaspoon soda, one of cream tartar, half cup milk, four eggs. Drop into buttered tins, sprinkle with sugar and cinnamon.

Gingerbread. 1. Sugar. Six cups flour, two cups sugar, one cup butter, one cup milk, teaspoon soda. Roll thin.

2. **Hard Sugar.** Three quarters pound sugar, same of butter, one and a half pounds flour, four eggs, ginger, small teaspoon soda. Roll very thin and bake on tin sheets.

3. **Maggie's.** One cup molasses, one-half cup butter and lard mixed, two-thirds cup sour milk, teaspoon soda, teaspoon ginger, five coffee cups flour. Mix as soft as you can roll.

4. **Molasses.** One cup molasses, one large tablespoon lard, teaspoon salt, teaspoon ginger, teaspoon soda dissolved in one-half cup of cold water, three scant cups flour.

5. One cup molasses, butter size of an egg, one egg, one-half cup sour milk, one and one-half cups

flour, one teaspoon soda, cloves, ginger. Beat molasses, egg and butter together, add flour gradually, alternating with the milk.

6. Simplest and Best. One cup molasses, one heaping tablespoon of shortening (butter and lard), one teaspoon salt, a little of all kinds spices, one teaspoon soda in one-half cup hot coffee. Flour for a soft batter.

Ginger. One cup molasses, one cup brown sugar, three-fourths cup lard or butter, three cups flour, one cup boiling water, two teaspoons soda, two eggs. Spice to taste. Boil molasses, sugar, flour and butter together, then add hot water and soda, lastly the eggs. Bake in a cool oven.

Ginger Puffs. One cup molasses, one cup sugar, one cup water, one-half cup butter, one egg, five cups flour, tablespoon soda, tablespoon ginger and cinnamon. Drop on tins and bake.

Ginger Snaps. One cup butter, one cup sugar, two cups molasses, one cup warm water, two teaspoons soda, four tablespoons ginger, roll thin, bake in hot oven.

2. One and a half pounds flour, one-half pound lard, one pint molasses, three teaspoons soda, dissolved in a little water, two tablespoons ginger, little salt. Rub flour and lard together, roll thin, cut in squares.

Gold. 1. Yolks of eight eggs, one tablespoon butter, four cups flour, one cup sweet milk, two cups sugar, teaspoon soda, two of cream tartar. Flavor with lemon.

2. One cup butter, two cups sugar, three cups flour, one cup sweet milk, one teaspoon cream tartar, one-half teaspoon soda, yolks six eggs and one whole egg; flavor with lemon. Use whites of two eggs for frosting.

Golden. Yolks of eight eggs, one cup sugar, two cups flour, one-half cup butter, one-half cup milk, one teaspoon cream tartar, half teaspoon soda. Flavor with vanilla.

Graham. One half cup butter, one and one-half cups sugar, one cup milk, three and a half cups pastry flour, one and one-half cups raisins stoned and chopped, one egg, one teaspoon soda, nutmeg. Sift sugar over the top and bake an hour and a half in a moderate oven.

Harrison. Two cups molasses, two cups butter, one cup milk, five cups flour, four eggs, two pounds chopped raisins, teaspoon soda. Spice to taste.

Henry. One-half cup of butter, two cups sugar, one cup milk, three and a half cups flour, three eggs, one teaspoon cream tartar, one-half teaspoon soda, one cup chopped walnuts, one cup currants. Flavor with lemon.

Hartford Election. Two and a half pounds butter, three pounds sugar, four and a half pounds flour, three pounds raisins, four eggs, one pint yeast, one quart milk, mix the butter and sugar as for pound cake; take one-half thus beaten and mix with flour, milk and yeast, and set it to rise over night. In the morning add the other half of sugar and butter, eggs, raisins and spices and let it rise again. Put in pans and let stand an hour before baking.

Hermits. One cup butter, one and a half cups sugar, one cup raisins, three eggs, teaspoon soda dissolved in a little milk, all kinds spice, flour to roll out.

Hickory-Nut. One cup butter, four cups flour, three cups sugar, one cup sweet milk, four eggs, teaspoon soda, one pint hickory nut meat, half pint raisins.

Ice Cream. Two cups coffee A sugar, one scant cup butter (melted just enough to make it soft), one cup milk, whites of eight eggs, three cups flour, three heaping teaspoons baking powder; sift your flour, roll your sugar; cream the sugar and butter, then add milk; then add one-third of eggs and one cup flour, then another one-third of eggs and cup flour, then last one-third eggs and last cup flour, then add baking powder last of all. After the dough is thoroughly mixed, if it runs off the spoon add another one-half cup flour. Grease your pans well, put two layers of paper in the bottom of the pans. Bake in three layers. When nearly cold trim all the brown part off, then ice. Icing:—Whites of three eggs, well beaten, nearly three cups powdered sugar (or one pound), three-fourths cup water; mix sugar and water, boil until the syrup will collect in the bottom of a cup of cold water; have the eggs in a dish and pour the hot syrup upon them slowly; stir constantly until nearly cold then add a teaspoon of vanilla. If the icing seems too hard add a little hot water, and if it sticks to the knife dip the knife in hot water. Very nice.

Imperial. One pound butter, one pound sugar, one pound chopped raisins, one-quarter pound citron, one pound flour, half pound blanched almonds put in whole, eight eggs, mace, and one glass of wine.

Jelly. Two and one-half cups sugar, one cup butter, one cup milk, four cups flour, three eggs, one teaspoon cream tartar, half teaspoon soda.

Jumbles. Three cups butter, three cups sugar, six eggs, one-third cup milk, half teaspoon soda, flour to roll easily. Scatter on sugar, cut in fancy shapes. This makes many and will keep well. Nice.

2. **Soft.** Two cups sugar, one cup butter, three eggs, two-thirds cup sour milk, half teaspoon soda, four heaping cupfuls flour. Drop them on a tin with a spoon some distance apart; if too thin add a little more flour.

Julia. One cup sugar, one-half cup butter, one-half cup sweet milk, two eggs, two cups flour, teaspoon cream tartar, half teaspoon soda, vanilla.

Lady. One-half cup butter creamed, add gradually one cup sugar, one-half cup milk, one-half cup corn starch, one cup flour, one even teaspoon baking powder, whites of four eggs. Flavor with almond and a drop of lemon.

Lemon Snaps. One cup butter, two cups sugar, one-third cup milk, three eggs, teaspoon soda, two teaspoons lemon.

Magic. One cup sugar, half cup butter, one and a half cups flour, three eggs, three tablespoons milk, half teaspoon soda, teaspoon cream tartar. Flavor with vanilla or nutmeg.

Marble. One-half cup butter, one cup sugar, one-half cup milk, one and three-fourths cups pastry flour, whites of four eggs, one-half teaspoon cream tartar, one-fourth teaspoon soda. In another dish mix one-half cup molasses, one cup sugar, one-half cup butter, two and one-half cups flour, one-fourth cup milk, yolks of four eggs, one teaspoon cinnamon, three-fourths teaspoon cloves, one teaspoon nutmeg, little mace, one-half teaspoon cream tartar, one-fourth teaspoon soda; put spices and cream tartar and soda in the flour; put a layer of dark mixture into the pan, then one of the light and alternate until all is used. Draw a fork through the sides and middle of the whole once.

Marbled Chocolate. One cup butter, two cups powdered sugar, three cups flour, four eggs, one cup sweet milk, half teaspoon soda, one teaspoon cream tartar. After this is well mixed take out one and one-half cups of it and mix with it enough chocolate previously melted in a few drops of hot water to give a dark color, then put in pans in separate layers and bake half an hour.

Marshall. Two and a half cups sugar, one cup butter, one cup milk, four cups flour, four eggs, teaspoon soda and one of cream tartar; bake in two sheets plain; for the third sheet, add two tablespoons molasses, one cup raisins, one cup currants, one-quarter pound citron, all kinds spices. Wet this sheet with the white of an egg and place between the light ones.

Molasses. 1. One cup molasses, two cups sugar, one-half cup butter or lard, teaspoon soda, one cup boiling water, salt and ginger. To be made soft and dropped from the spoon.

2. One pint molasses, six ounces butter, three well beaten eggs, one-half pint milk, one teaspoon soda; warm molasses enough to melt butter, dissolve soda in milk, mix, add eggs, thicken with flour to the consistency of pound cake. Flavor with lemon.

3. **Drop.** One cup molasses, one cup sugar, one cup warm water, teaspoon soda, flour enough to drop from a spoon, one tablespoon butter.

4. **Mrs. Clark's.** One cup sugar, one-half cup butter, two eggs, teaspoon cream tartar, half teaspoon soda, two cups flour, half cup milk.

Mother Hubbard. One and one-half cups sugar, one cup butter, two cups flour, five eggs, one-half teaspoon baking powder, cream butter and add flour a little at a time, cream together; beat eggs and sugar very lightly; put baking powder in the flour, one teaspoon vanilla. It is nice with a little mace.

Nice. One and one-half cups butter, one cup sugar, half cup milk, two cups flour, three eggs, teaspoon cream tartar, half teaspoon soda; beat the whites separately and add just before going into the oven. Bake thirty minutes.

Nut. One cup butter, two cups sugar, one cup milk, three and one-half cups flour, three eggs, one-half teaspoon soda, one teaspoon cream tartar, one pound English walnuts, one pound stoned raisins.

2. **Cream.** Three-fourths cup butter, two cups sugar, three and one-fourth cups flour, three even teaspoons baking powder, one cup milk, five eggs; bake in jelly cake tins. Make the filling as follows:— Whites of two eggs, one and one-half cups powdered sugar; put the eggs in a bowl, sprinkle in one tablespoon sugar; beat with a wire whisk five minutes, add the rest of the sugar gradually, a tablespoon at a time; when all is added and it is smooth and creamy, flavor and stir in three-fourths cup nuts chopped fine. Spread this icing between the layers; sprinkle each layer with nuts. Ice the top with plain icing and lay on whole or half nuts over all.

3. **Golden.** Cream three-fourths cup butter and one and one-half cups sugar together, add yolks of eight eggs, one whole egg beaten till thick, one-half cup milk, two cups of flour sifted with one and one-half teaspoons cream tartar, one-half teaspoon soda, two teaspoons brandy, one cup chopped nuts slightly floured. Bake in individual pans; frost with golden

frosting made as follows:—One yolk beaten slightly, one teaspoon wine; confectioners' sugar to make it stiff enough to spread.

Orange. Cream three-fourths cup butter, add slowly two cups sugar, and cream together; into three cups sifted pastry flour mix two teaspoons baking powder; add one tablespoon of the prepared flour to the butter and sugar, then add four eggs, one at a time without first beating, with a tablespoon of the flour before breaking in each egg; then add the remainder of the flour alternating with one cupful of milk. Flavor with orange. Bake about forty minutes in a moderate oven. ORANGE FROSTING:—Yolk of one egg, extract of orange, enough confectioners' sugar to make it thick enough to spread.

Plain Raisin. One-half cup molasses, one cup sugar, one half cup butter, one-half cup sour milk, teaspoon soda, two eggs; three cups flour. Raisins and spice.

Piccolomini. Three cups sugar, one cup butter, rub to a cream; beat five eggs very light, and stir gradually into the mixture together with four full cups flour and one of sweet milk. Dissolve in a little warm water half teaspoon soda, one teaspoon cream tartar, add nutmeg and wine glass rose water.

Pound. Rub one pound sugar and three-quarters pound butter to a cream, add the well beaten yolks of ten eggs, then the whites, and stir in gradually a pound of sifted flour.

Quick Cream Pie. Beat the whites of two eggs with one-half cup sugar, add the beaten yolks, two-thirds cup flour, one-half teaspoon cream tartar, one-fourth teaspoon soda (or one teaspoon baking powder).

Bake in a round tin. INSIDE:—One-half pint milk, one egg, one-half cup sugar, one-fourth cup flour; cook until thick and flavor as preferred.

Raised Loaf. One cup sugar (heaping), one-half cup butter, one egg, small piece of soda dissolved in a teaspoon of warm water, mace, cinnamon and nutmeg, two cups raised bread dough, one cup stoned raisins. Let it rise three hours before baking.

Rice Flour. One cup butter, one cup sugar, five eggs, two cups rice flour.

Rockland. One cup butter, two cups sugar, one cup milk, five eggs, half teaspoon soda, teaspoon cream tartar, four cups flour. Makes two loaves.

Sally Jewett. Three-quarters pound sugar, one-half pound butter, one cup molasses, one cup milk, five eggs, one pound flour, heaping teaspoon soda, one pound raisins, two tablespoons each cloves and cinnamon, one nutmeg, currants, citron, wine glass brandy.

Silver. Two cups of sugar, two and one-half cups flour, one-half cup butter, three-quarters cup milk, whites of eight eggs, teaspoon cream tartar, half teaspoon soda. Almond essence and chocolate frosting.

2. One and one-half cups sugar, one-half cup butter, three-fourths cup sweet milk, two cups flour, one teaspoon cream tartar, one-half teaspoon soda, whites of four eggs, well beaten; flavor with vanilla; bake in a slow oven.

Snow. One pound of sugar, three-quarters pound butter, one pound flour, whites of sixteen eggs, lemon or rose water.

Spice. One cup butter, one and a half cups sugar, two-thirds cup milk, three eggs, three cups flour, one teaspoon each kind of spice, one cup raisins, one teaspoon soda, citron and currants if you choose. Bake in roll pans.

Sponge. One cup sugar, one cup flour, four eggs, half teaspoon soda sifted in dry.

2. Three cups sugar, six eggs, one cup cold water, little salt, four cups flour, teaspoon soda, two teaspoons cream tartar; beat the yolks and stir into sugar until smooth, then add the whites beaten light, then cold water with soda, then flour with cream tartar, two teaspoons lemon put in last.

3. Four eggs, one cup sugar, one cup flour; beat the whites stiff, then the sugar must be well beaten into the whites, add next the yolks previously well beaten, and just as you are ready to put into the oven, stir the flour in. Very nice.

4. Eight eggs, scant two cups flour, one teaspoon mace, beat whites and yolks separately, then together, then stir in two cups sugar, and then flour. Bake in quick oven. Nice.

5. Beat eight eggs very light, add one pound sugar, twelve ounces flour. Flavor with lemon or almond. Drop them on tins with teaspoon, sift sugar over them and bake in a quick oven.

Trifles. One egg beaten thoroughly, one teaspoon salt, all the flour that can be kneaded in. Roll as thin as paper. Fry in hot lard.

Walnut. One cup butter, two cups sugar, three and a half cups flour, two-thirds cup milk, three eggs, one cup chopped raisins, one cup walnuts, half teaspoon soda.

Washington. One pound brown sugar, one-half pound butter, four eggs (well beaten), one cup milk (medium size cup), one pound flour sifted twice, one pound fruit mixed with flour, currants, raisins and citron, one wine glass wine, one nutmeg, teaspoon cinnamon, two tablespoons baking powder. Makes one large cake.

White. Whites of eight eggs, two cups sugar, one-half cup butter, three-quarters cup milk, three cups flour, one teaspoon cream tartar, half teaspoon soda. Bake in layers, spread each with icing and grated cocoanut, and when put together cover the whole with the icing and cocoanut.

2. One cup butter, two cups sugar, three and one-half cups flour, whites of five eggs, one cup milk, teaspoon cream tartar, half teaspoon soda. Flavor with almond.

White Mountain. One cup butter, two cups sugar, four eggs, three and a half cups flour, two-thirds cup milk, teaspoon cream tartar, half teaspoon soda, teaspoon extract of lemon. Bake in four thin sheets and when done put a layer of frosting between each sheet.

Boiled Icing. One cup granulated sugar, one-third cup boiling water, white of one egg, one saltspoon cream tartar; boil the sugar and water without stirring, until the syrup taken up on skewer will "thread" or "rope;" when it is nearly at that point, beat the egg stiff, add the cream tartar, and pour the boiling syrup over the egg in a fine stream, beating well, when it thickens and is perfectly smooth.

Caramel Frosting. 1. One cup sugar, one-half cup milk; flavor to taste; boil hard just six minutes.

2. **Chocolate.** Add one square of chocolate to the caramel frosting and boil a little longer. Flavor with vanilla.

Chocolate Frosting. 1. One cup milk, two cups sugar, one strip chocolate; mix and boil together eight minutes; then beat till thick enough to spread.

2. Beat the whites of two eggs to a stiff froth, add one and a one-half cups sugar, four tablespoons of chocolate.

Cocoanut Frosting. Beat the whites of five eggs to a stiff froth, add two cups of prepared cocoanut, and powdered sugar enough to make it sufficiently stiff to spread with a knife. Flavor with extract lemon, vanilla or almond. After spreading the frosting upon the cake, sprinkle a little dry cocoanut over it.

PICKLES.

"Peter Piper picked a peck of pickled peppers."

Bordeaux Sauce. Two gallons cabbage cut coarse, one gallon cut green tomatoes, one-half dozen onions sliced, two heads of cauliflower, broken in pieces, two heads celery, cut fine, eight green peppers cut in small pieces, one ounce whole allspice, one ounce whole black pepper, one-half ounce whole cloves, four tablespoons ground mustard, one pound sugar, one and one-half gills of salt, vinegar to not quite cover the whole. Mix, and boil slowly two hours.

Chili Sauce. Forty-eight ripe tomatoes, ten peppers, two large onions, two quarts vinegar, four tablespoons salt, two teaspoons each cloves, cinnamon, nutmeg and allspice, one cup sugar. Slice the tomatoes, chop peppers and onions together, add vinegar and spices, and boil until thick enough. Mustard and curry powder improves this.

2. Twelve ripe tomatoes, four green peppers, one large onion, one cup strong vinegar, tablespoon salt, three of sugar, one teaspoon each of all kinds spice. Cook till soft.

Chow-Chow. Two gallons green tomatoes, two white onions, one-half dozen green peppers, one dozen cucumbers, two heads cabbage, all chopped fine; let this stand over night with a teacup of salt sprinkled over it; in the morning drain off the brine, and season with one tablespoon of celery seed, one ounce turmeric, one-half teaspoon cayenne pepper, one cup brown sugar, one ounce cinnamon, one ounce allspice, one ounce black pepper, one-fourth ounce cloves, vinegar enough to cover. Boil one-half hour.

Cauliflower. Six heads cauliflowers, two and one-half quarts vinegar, two and one-half cups brown sugar, three eggs, one-half bottle French mustard, one tablespoon ginger, few garlics, about four, one green pepper, one-fourth teaspoon cayenne pepper, butter size of half an egg, one-half ounce turmeric; beat well together the egg, sugar, mustard, ginger and turmeric, then boil all the ingredients in the vinegar ten minutes; boil cauliflower in salt water until tender; then place cauliflower in jar and pour vinegar hot over it. Cut the cauliflower in pieces of convenient size.

Cucumber. Sprinkle small cucumbers with salt, then pour vinegar over them and let them soak twenty-four hours; scald in hot vinegar and put in jars when cold. If you wish put various spices, done up in a little bag in the vinegar.

Pure Grape. Four quarts grapes, four pounds sugar, one-half pint vinegar, one tablespoon ground cloves; squeeze the pulp from the skins, put the pulp in a kettle with water enough to keep from scorching, and boil until you can easily separate the seeds by rubbing through a coarse sieve; then put skins, pulp and juice together and boil fifteen minutes.

Hodge Podge. Two quarts chopped green tomatoes, two of onions, two green peppers, mix together; to the six quarts add one pint brown mustard seed, one cup salt; after standing three or four days, add good cider vinegar sufficient to cover it. Keep in dry place.

Mustard. Two quarts onions, two quarts pickled cucumbers, two quarts green tomatoes, two quarts red and green peppers, two heads of cauliflower, two or three heads of celery, chop and let stand in brine over night, then drain and scald in vinegar with a piece of alum size of a filbert; have only vinegar enough to cover the pickle. Cook until tender, draw off the vinegar. DRESSING:- One-fourth pound ground mustard, one-half ounce turmeric, one-half ounce celery seed, two cups sugar, one cup flour; stir into one gallon of boiling vinegar, let stand over the fire about three minutes, stirring constantly. Pour over the pickle while hot and bottle when cold.

Ohio Catsup. Take three dozen ripe cucumbers, eight white onions, peel them and chop as fine as possible; sprinkle over them one-half cup salt; put the whole into a sieve and let them drain eight hours; take one cup of mustard seed, one-half cup of pepper and mix together; put in a jar and cover with strong vinegar. Close tight, and let it stand three or four days, when it will be ready for use.

Pickle for Beef. Four gallons of water, five pounds salt, one and one-half ounces of saltpetre, two large spoons soda, two teacups molasses. Boil and skim, pour over beef when cold.

Pickle for Butter. Two quarts of salt, one quart sugar, one tablespoon saltpetre, two to four quarts of boiling water.

Pickle for Hams. One quart of salt, one pint molasses, one pound sugar, two ounces saltpetre. Hams may be kept in this pickle three or four weeks before smoking.

Pickle for Pork. Two quarts of salt, three pints molasses; four ounces saltpetre, two ounces cloves, ten quarts water.

Pickled Eggs. Boil one dozen of fresh eggs fifteen minutes, put them in cold water to cool, take off the shells and place them in a jar, cover them with good vinegar. These are nice for picnics.

Pickled Lemons. One dozen lemons, one-half cup salt, one onion cut fine, one nutmeg grated, one tablespoon allspice, one-half tablespoon ground cloves, one-half tablespoon ginger, one-half teaspoon cayenne pepper, one teacup white mustard seed, three teaspoons brown sugar. Score the lemons, put them into stone jars, alternating with the ingredients. Cover the whole with cider vinegar, put the jars into kettles of boiling water; boil four hours, then stop tightly, let them stand three months before using.

Pickled Oysters. Simmer the oysters in their own liquor; take out the oysters and into the liquor put pepper and salt, cloves and nutmeg to taste, boil up once and pour over the oysters. Cooked early in the morning, ready for dinner. Keep two or three days.

Pickled Peaches. 1. Seven pounds of peeled peaches, three and a half pounds sugar, one pint vinegar, cloves or root ginger for spice; boil and add fruit until scalded, then put in jars and pour the scalding liquor on and cover tightly.

2. To every quart of vinegar add one pound sugar; scald and pour hot over the peaches for six successive mornings.

Pickled Tongue. Take a corned beef tongue and boil until tender, take off the skin, put it into a stone basin or jar and cover it with good cider vinegar, add a few allspice, whole peppers and cloves, not more than one dozen of each.

Sweet Ripe Cucumber. Pare and slice ripe cucumbers and let them stand over night in very salt water. Take one gallon vinegar, one pound of brown sugar and spice for a syrup; use whole spice and let them remain; when the syrup is boiling put in the cucumbers, boil till done. This looks and tastes very nice.

Sweet Ripe Tomato. Seven pounds ripe tomatoes, three and one-half pounds sugar, one quart vinegar; spices—cloves, allspice and cinnamon; put the sugar and vinegar over the fire till melted; peel the tomatoes and put them in syrup, bags of cloves, allspice and cinnamon, each bag to be one and one-half inches square; when tomatoes are boiled skim them out and boil the syrup till quite thick. (Very nice).

Spiced Currants. Five pounds currants, four pounds brown sugar, one pint vinegar, two tablespoons cloves, two of cinnamon. Boil slowly two hours.

Sweet Piccalilli. Take tomatoes just turning, wash, and without paring, slice thick, put into a crock with salt, sprinkled between the layers and let stand over night. In the morning drain, and make a rich syrup of vinegar, sugar and spice, cinnamon, little mace and cloves; put a few of the tomatoes into the syrup and let them simmer slowly, take out before they are cooked to pieces and put into a crock, continue in this way until all are used. If the syrup gets too thin make fresh, pour over the tomatoes and cover tight.

Sweet Pickled Pears. One quart vinegar, three pounds brown sugar to six pounds pears; after the pears are peeled put them into cold water, and let them stand awhile, then steam until done; then stick three cloves in each pear. Boil syrup and drop the pears in.

Sweet Tomato. One peck green tomatoes, sprinkle on a little salt and let them stand over night, then strain off the water, put them in a kettle with enough vinegar to cover them, add half pound or quarter pound sugar, two cups white mustard seed, one-half cloves, one cup allspice and a little mace put in a bag. Six green peppers, six onions, cook three hours over a slow fire.

2. Seven pounds tomatoes, three pounds sugar, one quart vinegar, one ounce each cloves and cinnamon; boil three hours. Never ferments.

3. To one-half bushel green tomatoes (sliced), add one dozen large onions (sliced); scatter over the mixture one pound salt, and let it stand all night; in the morning drain off the brine; in four quarts water and two quarts of vinegar, cook tomatoes and onions together fifteen minutes; drain them again (this takes away the strong, rank flavor). Now to five quarts vinegar add four pounds brown sugar, four even tablespoons ground allspice and the same quantity of cloves, cinnamon, ginger and mustard, and one dessertspoon cayenne pepper; scald this mixture, and add the tomatoes, &c., letting all cook together ten or fifteen minutes just before removing from the fire. Stir in half pound whole white mustard seed. Very nice.

Tomato. Cut one peck green tomatoes in slices, and put in a stone jar, cover with one pint molasses; skim when it ferments, and your pickles are ready for use.

Tomato Ketchup. Take one bushel ripe tomatoes and five onions, boil until soft, squeeze through hair sieve, add one-half pint salt, one-quarter pound allspice, two ounces cloves, two ounces cayenne pepper, two tablespoons black pepper, two quarts vinegar; mix and boil three hours. This will fill twelve bottles.

JELLIES.

*"We must take the current when it serves,
Or lose our ventures."*

The surest way to clear jelly is to let the juice drain through a flannel bag without squeezing it.

The best and easiest way to cover jellies is to pour melted paraffine over them when they are quite cold. This hardens at once, when a piece of brown paper may be tied over the glass to keep out the dust. The cake of paraffine may be easily lifted off when the jelly is used, and if washed and put away can be melted and used another year. Paraffine is a clear white wax which is absolutely tasteless.

In making crabapple jelly put in the juice of one or more lemons according to the quantity so there will be an acid flavor, but not enough to taste of the lemon.

Apple. 1. Pare and cut into slices eighteen large acid apples, boil them in as much water as will cover them, when quite soft dip a coarse cloth into hot water, wring dry, and strain the apples through it. To one pint juice allow fourteen ounces sugar, add the peel of one lemon. Boil twenty minutes, take out the peel and put in jars.

2. One-half peck good tart apples, three pints water, boil until done enough to run a straw through them, then drain through a sieve; three-quarters pound sugar to one pint of juice. Boil twenty minutes.

Cider. One-half box gelatine with cold water sufficient to cover it, let it stand one hour, then add the grated rind and juice of one lemon, one-half pint or little more sugar, two-thirds pint of cider, pint and one-half boiling water, then strain into moulds.

Catawba Grape. Take fresh grapes, wash and pick from stems; put into porcelain kettle with enough water to keep from burning. Cook until seeds are clear. Drain through a jelly bag. To each pint of juice add one pint sugar. Boil till it strings.

Currant. Put the currants in a large preserving kettle without stemming them, and let them heat slowly; cook gently with frequent stirring, until fruit is well broken, will take perhaps three hours; squeeze them through a flannel bag; allow pound sugar to each pint of juice; return juice to the fire and boil twenty minutes, skimming frequently; then put in the sugar slowly, previously heated in the oven, so it will not stop the jelly from boiling; let the jelly come to a good boil, take it up and pour into glasses.

Orange. Dissolve one-half cup gelatine in one cup cold water; after standing one-half hour add a cup boiling water; drain this into the juice of twelve oranges, juice and grated rind of two lemons; sweeten with about two cups sugar. Strain.

Wine. 1. One box gelatine, one and one-half pints cold water, one-half pint good Sherry or Madeira wine, the peel of three lemons and their juice, nearly one pint white sugar, the beaten whites of three eggs, and the shells crushed; put it on the stove and stir very often, lest the gelatine should scorch; let it boil about five or ten minutes, then take scum and put it in your strainer to serve as a filterer. Pour in the jelly,

JELLIES. 97

and as fast as it runs out, pour back again until it is as clear as you wish.

2. One pint boiling water poured on one-third box gelatine, one cup sugar, one cup wine, one lemon, strain through muslin.

To Can Pineapples. Use quarter pound sugar to a pound of the cut pineapple; cut the pineapple in little squares or diamonds, put the sugar over it and let it stand over night; then pour off the juice, boil it till it thickens a little, pour over the fruit and boil it till the pineapple is tender.

Sweet Apple Preserve. Twelve pounds sweet apples, quartered and cored, six pounds sugar, one quart good vinegar. Dissolve sugar and vinegar, and cook apples in the syrup till done.

BEVERAGES.

"At one's cups."

Chocolate. One-eighth of a pound Baker's cooking chocolate dissolved in hot water, cook until it thickens; add one-third cup sugar, one quart boiling milk, let it boil slowly for five minutes, beating it as a scum will form; this is enough for a company of eight people at an afternoon tea.

Cream Soda. Three pounds white sugar, two ounces tartaric acid, three pints water, juice of one lemon. Boil five minutes, when nearly cold add the beaten whites three eggs, half cup flour mixed with the eggs, and half an ounce of checkerberry.

Currant Shrub. Put the currants in a porcelain kettle to heat, in order to extract the juice; to each pint juice add three-quarters pound white sugar; cook long enough to dissolve the sugar thoroughly; bottle and seal tight. This is a delicious drink when used with equal quantity of ice water.

Iced Tea. Early in the morning pour cold water on the tea, and let it stand all day; put in ice when ready to serve.

Lemonade for Picnics. Take a glass can of lemon juice and sugar, remembering that the juice of half a large lemon and three teaspoons sugar make a perfect glass of lemonade.

BEVERAGES.

2. Lemonade. A pleasant and healthy drink is made by putting the juice of one lemon in a glass of water, without sugar. This is good for billiousness.

3. Pineapple. Boil one cup sugar in one pint water ten minutes, cool slightly, and add one can grated pineapple and juice of three lemons; cool just before serving, add one quart ice water.

Mead. 1. Three pounds white sugar, five gills molasses, three pints water, four ounces tartaric acid, one-half ounce sassafras, same of checkerberry; boil and bottle.

2. Two pounds and one-half white sugar, two ounces tartaric acid, whites three eggs beaten to a froth, two quarts boiling water poured on the mixture; flavor with sassafras or lemon; cool and bottle. Three or four tablespoons to a tumbler filled two-thirds with water, stir in quarter teaspoon of soda. Drink quick.

Pop Beer. One pound sugar, one ounce cream tartar, ounce ginger, juice of two lemons, four quarts boiling water. When cold add a compressed yeast cake dissolved in a little water. Let it stand twenty-four hours and bottle.

Raspberry Vinegar. To ten quarts berries put one and one-half pints good vinegar, let them stand two nights; to each quart of juice, put one pound white sugar. Boil over a slow fire fifteen minutes, skim thoroughly and when cool bottle it.

Russian Tea. 1. When the water boils put in the tea, place the lid upon the teapot and put on the table to draw for a few moments, then pour into the silver teapot, leaving out the leaves.

2. Many like tea served with a thin slice of lemon in each cup, in the Russian fashion, instead of cream and sugar.

CANDIES.

"Sweets to the sweet."

Almond Cakes. Whites five eggs, stir in sugar enough to make it stiff, with just a little pinch of flour, half pound almonds scalded and pounded. Drop on buttered tins and bake in a quick oven.

Butter Scotch. 1. Two cups sugar, two tablespoons of water, butter the size of an egg. Boil without stirring until it hardens when dropped into water.

2. One tablespoon butter, two tablespoons sugar, two tablespoons water, three tablespoons molasses, one teaspoon vanilla; just before it is cooked enough, one-fourth teaspoon of soda. Pour in a shallow tin and crease in squares.

Chocolate Caramels. 1. One cup sugar, one cup molasses, one gill cream, piece butter size of an egg, quarter pound chocolate, cook until it ropes, pour on buttered tins and cut in squares just before it is cold.

2. One cup sugar, one-third cup milk, one square chocolate, one-half tablespoon butter; boil hard seven minutes; flavor with vanilla, turn into a shallow pan, and when hard enough cut into squares. Do not stir while boiling.

3. One-fourth pound chocolate, three cups brown sugar, one cup milk, piece butter the size of an agg; flavor with vanilla. Boil one-half hour.

4. Creamed Chocolate. Three cups sugar, one-half cake grated chocolate (Baker's), one cup milk, one-fourth cup butter, one teaspooon vanilla; boil just ten minutes; take off in a dish and beat until it sugars. Pour in pan, cool and then cut in squares.

Checkerberry Drops. One pint sugar, five tablespoons water, boil four minutes; two tablespoons sugar, half teaspoon cream tartar, fifteen drops oil of checkerberry stirred into mixture after boiling. Drop on tin or paper.

Chocolate Creams. The white of one egg, an equal quantity of water; flavor with vanilla; beat the egg to a froth, add water and vanilla, then stir in as much contectioners' sugar as will hold, roll into balls and drop into chocolate steamed over the tea-kettle.

Chocolate Drops. Two cups sugar, one-half cup water; boil three minutes, take from the fire and cool in a pan of water, stirring constantly till cold enough to roll into small balls; place them on buttered tins; take one-half bar chocolate, not sweetened, and break into small pieces and place in a plate over the tea-kettle; when this is melted, take the balls on a straw and roll in this chocolate. Flavor the cream and chocolate with vanilla.

Cocoanut. One-half pound sugar, two tablespoons water, one-half pound grated cocoanut; stir until boiled to a flake. Put in buttered tins and cut in squares when cold.

Cocoanut Drops. One cup prepared cocoanut, white of one egg beaten to a froth, one-half cup sugar, one spoonful flour; mix, then drop on buttered tins and bake five minutes in a quick oven. Flavor to taste.

Cream. One pint sugar, one-half pint water, one tablespoon vinegar; boil hard twenty minutes, but do not stir. Work in vanilla as you pull it.

Cream Walnuts. Into the white of an egg stir enough powdered sugar to roll into balls; flavor to suit the taste. Dip halves of English walnuts into a syrup made by boiling two tablespoons sugar and one tablespoon water three or four minutes; then place one-half walnut on either side of each ball and press together. Dates may be used in the same way.

Ice Cream. Two cups granulated sugar, scant cup water; as soon as this boils add one-fourth teaspoon cream tartar dissolved in water; then boil without stirring until brittle when dropped in water; add butter the size of a walnut just before taking from the stove; pour into a buttered dish to cool and pull as hot as possible until white. Flavor while pulling with lemon and vanilla.

Kisses. Whites four eggs, two cups sugar. Flavor as you please, drop on a tin covered with paper, and bake in a moderate oven.

Molasses. One pint molasses, one pound white sugar, large tablespoon vinegar, half coffee cup cold water, piece butter large as a walnut. Boil all together in a spider without stirring twenty minutes.

Orange Drops. Juice and grated rind of one orange, little lemon juice; stir in confectioners' sugar till stiff enough to roll out into balls. No cooking.

Peppermints. One cup sugar, one-half cup water, boil, stirring often, twenty minutes. Take from the stove and add half teaspoon cream tartar and peppermint to taste.

Taffy. 1. Six cups white sugar, one cup vinegar, one cup water; boil without stirring one-half hour; when done stir in one tablespoon soda dissolved in hot water. Flavor with vanilla and pull.

2. One-half pound brown sugar, three ounces butter, one and one-half cups cold water. Boil all together with the rind of one lemon, adding juice when done.

Stuffed Dates. One pound dates stoned, and filled with one-half pound peanuts salted, baked and then chopped up fine. After the dates are filled roll in granulated sugar.

CHAFING-DISH COOKING.

"To be good, be useful. To be useful, always be making something good."

Cheese Fondu. Put tablespoon butter in the chafing-dish; when melted, add cup fresh milk, cup of fine bread crumbs, two cups grated cheese, saltspoon of dry mustard, little cayenne. Stir constantly and add, just before serving, two eggs, beaten light.

Curried Fish. Cook one tablespoon of onion, cut very fine, in one tablespoon butter five minutes; be careful not to burn; mix one tablespoon curry powder with one tablespoon flour, and stir into the melted butter; add gradually one-half pint milk or cream, stirring constantly; then add a large cupful any kind of cold boiled fish; let it simmer a few minutes and serve very hot.

Lobster. Chop or shred the meat of a cold, boiled lobster, tail and claws; pour over it the juice of two lemons, add one-half teaspoon cayenne and a teaspoon salt; put in the chafing-dish three tablespoons fresh butter; when melted add the lobster. Let it simmer for about ten minutes stirring constantly.

Lobster a la Newburg. Take the nicest part of two small lobsters, cut into small pieces like dice, put into the chafing-dish with a tablespoon butter; season well with pepper and salt, pour over it a gill of wine; cook ten minutes; add the beaten yolks three eggs and half pint cream. Let all come to a boil and serve immediately.

Luncheon Sardines. Select firm, medium-sized sardines, remove skin carefully, put hot water dish on chafing-dish frame and pour into it pint of hot water; now put cutlet dish on top and into it put one teaspoon butter, one teaspoon lunch paste, one-half wine glass of wine and very little white pepper. In this warm up the sardines putting each one on toast and serve at once.

Oysters, Maitre d'Hotel. Dry dozen oysters in a napkin; put tablespoon butter in the chafing-dish, and when very hot place the oysters in single layers; when brown on one side turn them upon the other, and brown also; season with pepper and salt. Put out the lights, squeeze the juice of half a lemon over the oysters, strew over them very little chopped parsley and serve with or without toast.

Relish for Raw Oysters. Two tablespoons finely chopped white onion, one teaspoon English "made" mustard, one dozen drops of Tabasco sauce, one-half teaspoon salt, one tablespoon horse radish, one saltspoon white pepper, one gill strong white vinegar; mix, let stand a few minutes and put very little on each oyster.

Welsh Rarebit. Put a tablespoon butter in the chafing-dish; when nearly melted, add pound and one-half fresh cheese, cut small as dice, teaspoon dry mustard, little cayenne, stir all the time, add small amount of beer to prevent burning. Keep adding beer, about half pint in all. Serve hot on toast.

DISHES FOR INVALIDS.

Beef Tea. Fill glass can with lean beef cut in small pieces; cover closely and set in kettle of cold water, let this come to a boil, and boil till the juice is all extracted.

Infant's Beef Tea. Three ounces each beef and veal; boil six hours in water having a quart when it is done, add salt and skim when cold. Take equal parts of milk, water and broth, boil a minute and sweeten if desired.

Chicken Tea. Remove skin and fat from a chicken, cut in small pieces; boil in one quart water, with a little salt, for twenty minutes. Pour off the tea before the meat is quite cold.

Baked Milk. Bake two quarts milk eight or ten hours in a moderate oven in a jar covered with writing paper tied down. It will be thick like cream. Good for weak persons.

Eau Sucre. Dissolve three or four lumps loaf sugar in a glass of ice water, and take teaspoon every four minutes for a "tickling in the throat," or hacking cough.

Lemon Moss. Put a few sprigs of moss, which has been well washed, to soak in water enough to make the drink the thickness of cream. After standing a short time, add lemon juice and loaf sugar.

Toast Water. Slices of toast, nicely browned, without a symptom of burning; enough boiling water to cover them; cover closely and let them steep till cold; strain the water, sweeten to taste, and cool with ice. A bit of lemon juice can be added.

INDEX.

BREAD.

Bangor Corn Cake,	6	Muffins, Indian Meal,	8
Bannock,	3	Muffins, Raised,	9
Batter,	3	Muffins, Rye,	9
Blueberry Cake,	3	Muffins, White,	9
Breakfast,	3	Pancakes,	9
Breakfast Puffs,	4	Parker House Rolls,	9
Brown Bread,	4	Potato Biscuit,	9
Buckwheat Cakes,	4	Potato Cakes,	10
Buns,	4	Potato Rolls,	10
Buns,	5	Quaker Biscuits,	10
California Biscuit,	5	Rice Crumpets,	10
Cheese Sandwiches,	5	Rusks,	11
Corn Cake,	5	Raised Rye Bread,	11
Corn Cake,	6	Raised Rye Biscuit,	11
Corn Bread,	6	Rye Rolls,	11
Egg Pop-Overs,	6	Squash Biscuit,	11
Flannel Cakes,	6	Squash Fritters,	11
French Toast,	7	Squash Gems,	11
Fried Biscuits,	7	Squash Griddle Cakes,	12
Graham Bread,	7	Steamed Whole Wheat Loaf,	12
Graham Rolls,	7	Tea Rolls,	12
Huckleberry Biscuit,	7	Waffles,	12
Indian Breakfast Cake,	7	Waffles, German,	12
Indian Cake,	7	Wheat Gems,	12
Indian Drop Cake,	8	White Corn Cake,	6
Muffins,	8	Yeast,	13
Muffins, English,	8		
Muffins, Graham,	8		

SOUPS.

Black Bean,	16	Mock Oyster,	17
Beef,	16	Noodle,	17
Bouillon,	16	Pea,	18
Celery,	17	Potato,	18
Corn,	17	Stock,	16
Lobster,	17	Tomato,	18

FISH.

Baked Cod,	21	Lobster Croquettes, .	23
Baked Fish,	21	Oyster and Clam Fritters,	23
Baked Lobster,	21	Oysters, Broiled, . .	23
Baked Shad Roe,	22	Oysters, Roast, .	23
Devilled Crabs,	22	Oysters, Scalloped, .	24
Escaloped Oysters,	22	Potted Shad, .	24
Fillets of Halibut, .	22		
Fish Balls, . .	22	Salmon Croquettes,	24
Fish Croquettes,	23	Tomato Sauce, .	22

MEATS.

Camelons, .	29	Potted Beef, . . .	27
Croquettes, .	27	Roast Lamb and Mint Sauce,	28
Devilled Ham, . .	28	Sausages, ...	28
How to choose Meats,	27	Suet, to Chop . . .	29
Meat Pie, . . .	28	Timbales, .	29
Meat and Potted Pie,	28	Veal Cutlets, .	29
Minced Veal, . .	29	Veal Loaf, . .	29

FOWL.

Chicken Pie, .	30	Pressed Chicken, .	31
Chicken Croquettes,	31	Potted Pigeons,	32
Chicken in Jelly,	30	Roast Duck, .	31
Maryland Chicken, .	31	Turkey. .	32

EGGS.

A la Cream,	36	Egg Vermicelli,	35
Baked Eggs, .	36	Omelette, .	35
Dropped Eggs,	36	Shirred Eggs, .	36

SALADS.

Cabbage, . .	38	Mustard Dressing,	41
Chicken or Lobster,	38	Salad Dressing, .	39
Dressing for Cabbage,	39	Salad Dressing, . .	40
Dressing for Salad, .	39	Salad Dressing, Bangor, .	40
Dressing for Lobster Salad,	39	Salad Dressing Cream,	40
Egg Salad, . . .	38	Welsh Rarebit, .	41
Leontine's Dressing,	39		

PIES.

Apple Custard,	47	Mince Meat,		46
Bambury Tart,	47	Mock Mince.		46
Chess,	44	Modern Rhubarb.		47
Cocoanut,	44	Orange,		46
Cream,	44	Pie Crust,		44
Cream Raspberry,	47	Pie Crust Glaze, ,		44
Lemon,	45	Rhubarb,		47
Marlborough,	45	Saratoga,		47
		Squash,		46

PUDDINGS.

Almond Rice,	53	Fruit,	55
Apple,	48	Fruit Salad,	55
Apple Charlotte,	48	Indian,	50
Apple Cream,	48	Lemon Jelly,	54
Apple Meringue,	53	Mountain Dew,	51
Caramel Custard,	54	Orange Cream,	52
Carrot,	52	Pineapple,	52
Charlotte Russe,	48	Prune Whip,	53
Chocolate,	49	Queen of Puddings,	51
Coburg,	54	Rye,	51
Cocoanut,	50	Scarboro Puffs,	51
College,	49	Snow Balls,	53
Columbia,	49	Sponge,	51
Cottage,	49	Strawberry Trifle,	55
Cracker,	49	Tapioca Cream,	52
English Plum,	50	Tipsy Trifle,	54
Fig,	53		

SAUCES.

Sauce,	58	Mollie's Pudding,	58
Foaming Sauce,	59	Plain Pudding,	58
For Whipped Cream,	59	Raspberry Foam,	59
Hard Sauce,	58	Wine,	59

FROZEN DISHES.

Arrowroot Ice,	60	Delicious Ice Cream,	61
Bisque Glace,	60	Frozen Pudding,	61
Cafe Parfait,	60	Fruit Ice Cream,	62
Caramel,	60	Ice Cream,	61
Chocolate Cream,	61	Ice Creem,	62
Coffee Cream,	61	Ice Cream, Strawberry,	62

Lemon Ice,	63	Velvet Cream,		63
Lemon Sherbets,	63	Walnut Bisque,		64
Orange Water Ice,	63	Water Ice,	.	64

CAKE.

Almond, . . .	65	Doughnuts, Aunt Grant's,		73
Almond Silver, .	65	English Walnut,	.	73
Almond or White, .	66	Feather,	. .	73
Angel, . . .	66	Fig, ...		74
Blueberry, . .	66	Filling for a Layer Cake,		74
Boiled Icing, . .	85	French, . . .		74
Boston Ginger Bread, .	66	French Loaf, . .		74
Boston Puffs, . .	66	Fruit, . . .		74
Bread, . . .	66	German, . . .		75
Bride's, . . .	67	Gingerbread, Sugar, .	.	75
Bridgewater, .	67	Gingerbread, Hard Sugar,		75
Caramel, . .	67	Gingerbread, Maggie's, .		75
Caramel Frosting, .	85	Gingerbread, Molasses,	.	75
Chocolate, . .	67	Gingerbread,Simplest and Best,		76
Chocolate Cocoanut, .	68	Ginger, . . .		76
Chocolate Frosting, .	86	Ginger Puffs, . .		76
Citron, . . .	68	Ginger Snaps, .		76
Clove, . . .	68	Gold, . . .		76
Cocoanut, . .	68	Golden, . .		77
Cocoanut, . . .	69	Graham, . .		77
Cocoanut, One, Two, Three, Four, . . .	69	Harrison, . . Hartford Election, .		77 77
Cocoanut Cream, . .	69	Henry, . . .		77
Cocoanut Frosting, . .	86	Hermits, . . .		77
Cold Water, . .	69	Hickory-Nut, . .		77
Composition, . .	69	Ice Cream, . .		78
Cookies, . . .	70	Imperial, .		78
Cookies, Cocoanut, . .	70	Jelly, . . .	.	78
Cookies, Molasses, .	70	Jumbles, . .	.	78
Cookies, Rice Flour, .	71	Jumbles, Soft, .	.	79
Cookies, Soft Molasses, .	70	Julia, . . ,	.	79
Cookies, Sugar, .	71	Lady, . . .	.	79
Corn Starch, .	71	Lemon Snaps, .	.	79
Cream, . . .	71	Magic, . .	.	79
Cream Cakes, . .	71	Marble, . . .		79
Crullers, . .	72	Marbled Chocolate, .	.	80
Crumpets, . .	72	Marshall, . .	.	80
Currant, . . .	72	Molasses, . .	.	80
Dayton, . . .	72	Molasses Drop, .	.	73
Delicate, . . .	72	Molasses Drop, .	.	80
Delicious, . . .	72	Molasses, Mrs. Clark's,	.	80
Delicious, . . .	73	Mother Hubbard, .	.	80
Doughnuts, . .	73			
Doughnuts, Aunt Caroline's,	73			

Nice,	81	Rockland,	83
Nut,	81	Sally Jewett,	83
Nut, Cream,	81	Silver,	83
Nut, Golden,	81	Snow,	83
Orange,	82	Spice,	83
Plain Raisin,	82	Sponge,	84
Piccolomini,	82	Trifles,	84
Pound,	82	Walnut,	84
Quick Cream Pie,	82	Washington,	84
Raised Loaf,	83	White,	85
Rice Flour,	83	White Mountain,	85

PICKLES.

Bordeaux Sauce,	89	Pickled Eggs,	92
Cauliflower,	90	Pickled Lemons,	92
Chili Sauce,	89	Pickled Lemons,	92
Chow-Chow,	89	Pickled Oysters,	92
Cucumber,	90	Pickled Peaches,	92
Cucumber, Sweet Ripe,	93	Pickled Tongue,	92
Hodge Podge,	90	Pure Grape,	90
Mustard,	90	Spiced Currants,	93
		Sweet Piccalilli,	93
Ohio Catsup,	91	Sweet Pickled Pears,	93
Pickle for Beef,	91	Tomato,	94
Pickle for Butter,	91	Tomato Catsup,	94
Pickle for Ham,	91	Tomato, Sweet Ripe,	94
Pickle for Pork,	91	Tomato, Sweet,	94

JELLIES.

Apple,	95	Orange,	96
Cider,	96	To Can Pineapple,	97
Catawba Grape,	96	Sweet Apple Preserves,	97
Currant,	96	Wine,	96
Directions for Making,	95	Wine,	97

BEVERAGES.

Chocolate,	98	Mead,	99
Cream Soda,	98	Pineapple,	99
Currant Shrub,	98	Pop Beer,	99
Iced Tea,	98	Raspberry Vinegar,	99
Lemonade for Picnics,	98	Russian Tea,	99
Lemonade for Picnics,	99		

CANDIES.

Almond Cakes,	100	Cream Walnuts,		102
Butter Scotch,	100	Ice Cream,		102
Caramels, Chocolate,	100	Kisses,		102
Caramels, Creamed Chocolate,	101	Molasses,		102
Checkerberry Drops,	101	Orange Drops,		102
Chocolate Creams,	101	Peppermints,		102
Chocolate Drops,	101	Stuffed Dates,		103
Cocoanut,	101	Taffy,		103
Cocoanut Drops,	101			
Cream,	102			

CHAFING-DISHES.

Cheese Fondu,	104	Luncheon Sardines,	105
Curried Fish,	104	Oysters, Maitre d'Hotel,	105
Lobster,	104	Relish for Raw Oysters,	105
Lobster, a la Newburg,	104	Welsh Rarebit,	105

DISHES FOR INVALIDS.

Baked Milk,	106	Infant's Beef Tea,	106
Beef Tea,	106	Lemon Moss,	106
Chicken Tea,	106	Toast Water,	106
Eau Sucre,	106		

www.ingramcontent.com/pod-product-compliance
Lightning Source LLC
Chambersburg PA
CBHW020141170426
43199CB00010B/842